CONVERTING

CLICKS
— INTO —
PATIENTS

Building A Better Weight Loss Practice

**The Ultimate Guide To Leveraging
The Power of Online Marketing To
Win New Patients**

By **Tim McGarvey**

ISBN: 978-1-09832-457-5

Published in the United States of America

Special discounts are available on quantity purchases by corporations, associations, educators, and others. For details, contact the publisher at the above listed address

This book is dedicated to my wife who hopes she will somehow get a dog out of this book. Thank you, Julie.

Table of Contents

Introduction

As a medical practitioner it's your job to keep others healthy. But, that's getting harder and harder to do, and still make a profit. Is your practice growing and thriving?

In today's digitally fueled world, running a healthy medical practice means understanding online marketing principles as well as medical knowledge. Marketing a weight loss practice has unique challenges. A few tasks can be taken care of by a physician's assistant or office staff. However, the idea that you can post a few ads on Facebook or Instagram, or put a video up on YouTube, and get hundreds of new patients to call is a myth.

Building a successful weight loss practice today requires a mastery of digital marketing. SEO is harder than it seems and takes more time than you realize. Most practices we encounter have taken one of two approaches. Either they're attempting a superficial in-house marketing plan, or they've hired an expensive full-service marketing agency.

DIY means creating your own marketing message, creating a mishmash of platforms, and putting out ads once in a while. This won't get you the reach that is required, and doesn't bring in new patients. You can hire a full service agency and pay them dearly. For tens of thousands of dollars you can get a sleek website and customized advertising platforms and campaigns. This gobbles up tons of working capital, and still no measurable results. Some medical practitioners have tried both routes, and saw no new patients as a result. Now, these practitioners feel "stuck," and neglect to do any marketing at all.

There is a better way. Outlined here is a hybrid approach using traditional marketing principles and proven online strategies. These are the techniques and technologies I use to build successful weight loss practices around the U.S. And, they can be used to build your practice as well.

All of the principles in this manual have stood the test of time, because they work. This is a road map loaded with vital information and valuable links that are constantly updated. Just look for boxes marked "Free Resources," and stay up to date on the latest trends.

One word of caution: A road map is useful, but won't get you very far if you don't get behind the wheel. The key to successfully marketing a weight loss practice isn't only in the ideas, it's in the implementation. Use this guide consistently and before long your practice will be bustling. Lead more patients to better health, own a profitable practice, and experience the freedom that comes from knowing how to get new patients. Isn't that the goal? Then, be sure to share your success story with us.

Now, let's get started.

Chapter 1: New Patients & Profitability

How the Internet Can Fuel Your Medical Practice

Congratulations! By reading this guide, you are already one step ahead of the competition in your market. That's because most medical practices, including weight loss doctors, fail to promote themselves online effectively. Why do so many neglect this? For one thing, some doctors just don't believe that the Internet is a useful tool for marketing to bring in new patients. Others know that it is, but they don't have a clue how to get started. Or, perhaps as physicians, maybe they feel it's beneath them to have to market their practice. Having medical expertise should be enough, right?

Bravo for being brave enough to access this valuable guide.

How people research services, find practitioners and make decisions about their medical health care has changed a great deal in the last decade. This guide is for any doctor who understands that. Any practitioner seeking a steady stream of new patients will find that online marketing is crucial to establishing a thriving medical practice.

Our guide lays out a clear path to launching and marketing a medical practice that focuses on weight loss, which generates income without the headache of insurance administration. This business model brings an increasing number of new patients into the practice every month and guarantees recurring and referral patient visits. Help people live happier, healthier lives, and direct a busy medical practice. We'll show you how.

This book will change the way you think about medical weight loss, online marketing, and the best way to build a profitable, healthy practice.

Who's Searching Online?

Who searches for medical services online? The answer might surprise you. Everyone.

A study conducted by the research firms BIA/Kelsey and ComStat found that a staggering 97% of consumers conduct research online before purchasing a product or service. This means that any medical practice that doesn't show up in online search results loses out on this new patient traffic. If your practice doesn't pop up when a potential new customer conducts their online search, you will lose them to a nearby practice that does.

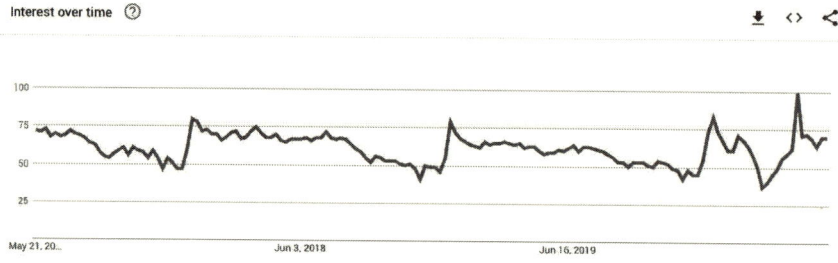

Search Term Volume "Weight Loss" 2017-2020

Not to be alarmist, but physicians must face the truth about how important the Internet is when building a healthy medical practice. The majority of people looking for help with services, including weight loss, prefer searching online over reading print ads or responding to a TV or radio commercial. The Internet is an accessible and convenient method for gathering information to make decisions.

Think about your browsing habits. How often do you use a print version of the Yellow Pages, or a printed piece like a newspaper or flyer when shopping? If you need a product or service, do you run to find a phone book or catalog? Or, do you Google it? I think we all know the answer.

Despite this, right now, medical practices spend more on print ads than online marketing. This doesn't make much sense. We've had clients tell us they've spent upwards $20,000 on print advertising, and got no online traffic, or new patient (foot) traffic. What a colossal waste of money. Traditional advertising methods, such as Yellow Page listings or TV commercials, can't be relied upon to bring in new business, and certainly not enough to justify the expense.

Businesses that track their return on investment (ROI) from print campaigns tell us that, year after year, they have seen diminishing returns. The data shows that every month, without fail, more and more people use Google or their favorite search engine to research their medical issues and find a reputable practitioner. Online marketing isn't a passing trend. It's a powerful way to tap into the Internet, which is a vast ocean of opportunity.

Together, we can drastically improve the results you gain from your marketing efforts, as we put your business in front of an entirely new audience. These will be people who are pre-qualified and already looking for the weight loss services you provide.

A Big Business Myth Buster

I'd like to address one of the most crucial online marketing myths, the belief that big business dominates search engine rankings with paid advertising. Many local practices believe they can't compete with big companies online, but this isn't true. Local practices can easily compete in this competitive arena, without spending a lot of money. Why?

Google has made significant changes to its search algorithm that favors local businesses. It's known as "local search return." Brick and mortar businesses that register properly with Google Places and Google + Local gain an advantage in rankings that they didn't have before. This feature used to be available on the Google Maps service only. Now, it's a tool available more broadly.

What is "local search return?" When people search online, businesses pop up in the Google Maps section. For example, if someone types in "Women's Shoes," the Google interactive map (a boxed-in area with a map), appears. It used to be that nationally known companies and brands would flood search results. The map, however, includes local businesses. There are even helpful markers that show the locations for the few businesses that show up in the box. It's important to remember that only those that register properly with Google show up.

Restaurants and hotels were the first companies to take advantage of this feature. It's a natural fit because visitors to a new city need to know where to eat, sleep, or find entertainment. The Google Maps box is such a useful tool that more local businesses are registering to be included. Google then thought, perhaps, people would want to see local products and services in their global search results as well? When Google realized that the answer was yes, people searching did want to see local results mixed in with main results, they adjusted. Now, Google's algorithm factors in local businesses.

Before this change, the primary index wasn't map-based. In other words, geographical location did not figure into global search results, only in the maps box. After typing in a phrase, millions of global returns used to flood the top results, which meant local businesses were pushed way down, never to be seen. This wasn't useful, or fair, for local businesses. And it wasn't helpful for people who were searching for local products and services. Thankfully, Google decided to incorporate local information into main search results. Local companies and practices can now rank higher, and alongside larger companies with more money to spend.

Today, anyone searching for a brick & mortar business in the main search bar will see a returns map with up to seven marked locations that are local. This is excellent news for your practice! You now have a much better chance of getting your local service business ranked side-by-side with bigger competitors. Even if you are competing with a giant company, like Amazon or Wikipedia, you can show up in the top results if you implement a comprehensive online strategy. This wasn't possible for a long time, so it's something many marketers have missed. What a tremendous benefit for your practice!

The screenshot above proves how powerful this local search return feature is. In the past, it was next to impossible to compete with search returns pulled globally. Now, local practices can come out on top because Google is weighting and incorporating local results.

Pro Tip: One word of caution: Getting into the top three to five spots is still not easy. It requires hard work and Internet savvy to compete with other local practices vying for visibility. Having a website with a few keywords isn't going to be enough. If you hire someone that doesn't truly understand the search engine algorithms, your practice might not show up, or worse, they'll use unfair tactics like SPAM that will get your business account banned.

There are legitimate methods of marketing online, and those are the ones outlined in this book. If executed carefully, these techniques can bring incredible results; hundreds of new patient calls every month. You'll have a shot at hitting the first, second, or third slot of organic (unpaid) listings with five-star reviews that draw potential new patients to your practice.

Google Rules

Warning: We've mentioned that Google changes its algorithms. One of these changes involves duplicate content, which is now more dangerous than ever!

Google's goal is to reward local businesses that offer high-quality services and products in their communities. However, they are cracking down on marketing sharks that try to game the system. Shortcuts include using cut-and-paste content or creating a gazillion fake listings. These tricks might work, but often they don't. Even if the underhanded tactics spark some interest, it's short-lived. And, if caught, your practice could get its account suspended. Using an untrained marketing person or attempting DIY marketing without understanding these complicated rules could lead to a Google suspension. If delisted, your practice might never recover search results again.

If this sounds harsh or unreasonable, keep in mind that Google is striving to help smaller practices like yours rise to the top in a vast ocean of global information. They are aggressively going after scammers and spammers so that you, a hard-working, local medical practice, can be found by people searching for the services you provide.

Be wary of any marketing consultant who says it's easy or cheap to get ranked in the top search results. It isn't. A successful online marketing strategy requires coordination and effort. It must go beyond using a few keywords and posting pre-packaged content. Unfortunately, this is still the norm for many digital marketing agencies, cutting corners instead of putting in the hard work that is necessary. I work with many clients who have fallen victim to schemes, unknowingly paying for recycled or stolen content, fake reviews, or SPAM that doesn't reflect the professionalism of their practice. This has gotten them into trouble with Google, and it has made potential new patients question their integrity. Not only did they NOT receive rankings from Google or show up search results, they got suspended and lost their opportunity to use online traffic to get new patients.

Being ignored by the search engines is the best-case scenario if someone you hire puts out plagiarized garbage or SPAM. In most cases, businesses are suspended, which means never showing up under that business name again. I advise you strongly not to take what seems like the easy way out because it's less expensive. Quality content and a well-designed online presence is at the core of any successful digital marketing strategy. That will never change. Creating it doesn't have to be hard, but it is time-consuming. It requires skill, patience, and discipline.

A high ranking and showing up on the first page of search engine results means correctly following a specific protocol. Here are just a few of the rules people break to try and game the system:

Don't steal, use duplicate content, or a link farm. Google has caught on to this trickery, and those employing these tactics are rapidly disappearing from search engine results. Don't be scammed by low ball marketing offers. If the proposal seems crazy cheap, it's probably not Google approved and won't work. Ask your marketing vendor where your content is going to come from. Will it be original to your business or duplicated and rehashed from another site? Where will the content appear? If they hesitate or don't have clear answers, say no thank you. And then, follow the instructions in this book. With some time, effort, and careful planning, you can create original content and use it to show up at the top of search results.

Just The Facts:

- The Internet is no longer optional. Most people are using it to find businesses and needs: You need to leverage it!

- Search is the big player now in Internet marketing. You need to make sure your page ranks high in the list of results when users search!

- Be very careful of how you enter the search engine market! A substandard presence online can be worse than no presence at all

- If you need help, make sure to choose your marketers carefully! Some may attempt underhanded tricks to boost you in the search rankings (like duplicate content), but these tricks can often carry severe penalties from the search engines for trying to game the system!

Chapter 2: Starting With The Right Strategy

Building, Managing and Marketing Your Reputation

Reputation management and reputation marketing are services that can truly transform a business and help it grow. However, the idea of reputation management is not clearly understood by most practice owners. If you intend to read only one chapter in this book, it should be this one. Reputation Marketing is where many practices fail, and it's how some succeed.

Most patients decide whether or not to call a practice based on the reviews they read online. This is where a new patient begins the decision-making process. It is vitally important that the reviews they read online are REAL reviews written by actual patients. Reviews can't be ones that you have written for yourself, or by someone you have hired. It doesn't work. Everyone instinctively knows when they are reading a fake review. Google knows, too. And, so do your potential new patients. Put in the time and effort to get real reviews from actual patients, and you'll hear from new people every day.

Get this FREE Guide to Earning a 5-STAR Reputation Online: http://build-five-star-reputation.com

Reputation Management

Reputation Management is the process of managing what is happening with your online reviews as they come in. It includes monitoring new reviews that show up, notifying the practice when they come in, and whether they are positive or negative. This allows owners an opportunity to respond quickly if a patient is frustrated by the experience they've had when visiting the practice. When practices follow up with any patient that has left a poor review, people tend to take their comments down once they feel they have been heard.

Our servers monitor directories, social networks, and search results 24 hours a day, tracking all of the new information being created and shared about the practice online. All of the information we find gets reported to the practice in real-time, and in our monthly reports.

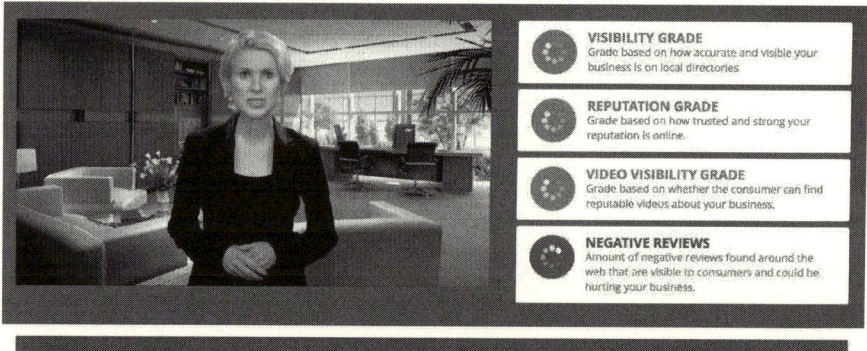

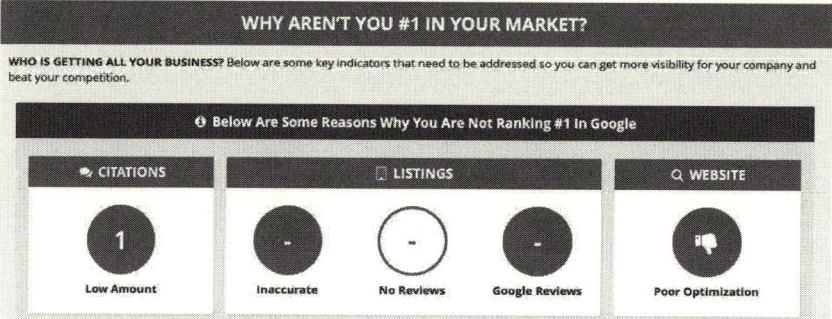

Free Report Checks Reviews and Directory Listings

Check Dozens Of Local Review Sites And Find Out What Your Patients Are Saying About You For FREE: http://weight-loss-analysis.com

Reputation Management is an incredibly valuable service. It only takes three bad reviews to see a significant downturn in inbound calls. Six bad reviews can close a business. In many cases, bad reviews show up, and the practice doesn't know they are out there. This downward spiral can be reversed by adding new, authentic reviews from real patients, another valuable aspect of Reputation Management.

Reputation Building

Reputation building is where we help weight loss practices request and receive new reviews from patients. And then, we leverage the presence of those reviews to generate more new patient phone calls.

There are three steps we take to help clients collect and market their reviews.

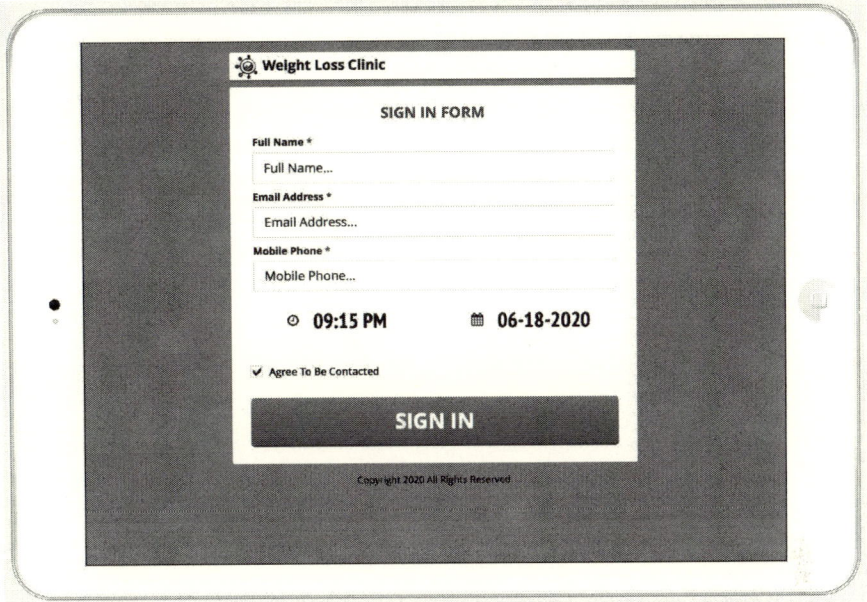

I-Pad Sign-In Form Starts the Review Process

First is a patient sign-in form. As patients arrive, they can sign-in on an iPad, which gives the practice permission to contact them by email and text. Once the patient signs in, the review process begins. If the practice is large and busy, the front desk can also use the sign-in system to text the patient when the doctor is ready to see them. Later, about four hours after the appointment is over; our smart system sends the patient an email or a text asking them about their experience. We ask several questions and inquire whether they would recommend the practice to family and friends. The patient is asked to give the practice a one to five-star rating.

Patients that rate their experiences with a four or five-star rating are sent ahead to a page asking them to leave a brief review on one of several review sites (Google, Yelp, Facebook. Vitals, etc.). If the patient rates their experience as less than four stars, we direct them to a feedback page. Here, they answer a few questions so we can understand their disappointment. When this happens, the staff immediately receives an email, letting them know that the patient has not had a great experience. The business is offered the chance to follow-up with the patient, ideally before they leave their negative comments on some review site.

This smart, automated email system allows us to follow-up with patients in an unobtrusive way for several days. If they do not reply to the original request for feedback, or start to leave feedback without completing the process, we reach out.

This is a powerful system, far more effective than a single email asking for a review. There is also the added advantage of using this system to obtain permission from the patient to use their review on your website or social media channels. This is a great way to market a practice. Patients can also leave feedback and reviews using a feedback page we include on the practice website. Patients will find this form when they read about the practice online, see reviews that other patients have left, and be inspired to add positive comments.

We provide review oriented business cards that staff can give to patients after their appointment. This is if the sign-in form isn't being used. The card asks the patient about their experience at the practice and sends them to a feedback page where they can leave their comments.

Get Five 5-Star Reviews in Five Days FREE
http://weight-loss-five-stars.com

Reputation Marketing

Once a patient leaves a positive review, it is syndicated to social media sites, and we share it on major online directories, like Google, Bing, Yahoo, and Yelp.

Our process doesn't end with syndicating reviews. We use them to create more new content, and we make sure the entire world sees those new reviews in different formats.

The first type of content we create is visual. We take text from the review and create an image that includes a quote from the review. This image, along with a caption and link back to the website, becomes a social media post. If the weight loss clinic has an offer for first-time patients, we often link from the review back to the new patient offer. We use the image and review to draw curious prospects in so we can show them the offer for new patients. These review images can be shared on all the online properties and platforms associated with the weight loss clinic.

60 Second Review Commercial with Spokesmodel Host

We do more than create images for social posting, we also use new reviews to create 60-second commercials with professional spokesmodel hosts. These videos are added to the company website and get shared on all the social media websites.

Get A 60 Second Professional Commercial Hosted By A Spokesmodel FREE: http://weight-loss-reputation-commercial.com.

We go farther than most with patient reviews and videos, by connecting the images, video commercials, and reviews with press releases. Press releases remain a fixture in the new industry. These press releases can be powerful tools used in the right way and over the right amount of time. All of this new content is pulled together and distributed to hundreds of new media sites, far and wide, announcing the review and telling prospects about the weight loss clinic and new patient offer.

Reputation Marketing is a powerful tool that creates a trustworthy and highly visible reputation for the practice online. We help practices position themselves as leaders in their city for weight loss services. Using this technique to its fullest can mean the difference between a thriving practice, or a stalled business that isn't growing.

Most doctors and small practices miss the value of requesting, publishing, and syndicating reviews online. Or they fall for superficial tactics, agents that create fraudulent reviews from non-existent patients and then fill their Google My Business pages with fake reviews. People know when reviews are not real. This also means missing out on the opportunity to hear about the patient's experience at the practice and using it to improve customer service.

Genuine reviews from actual patients are the best way to market a practice.

Test Drive Our Complete Reputation Services FREE for 90 days: http://weight-loss-reputation.com

Chapter 3: The Perils of A Pretty Website

Getting New Patients With the RIGHT Site

Now that you understand the importance of your reputation, your practice ranked by search engines, and the potential it has to reach new weight loss clients, it's time to build an online hub from the ground up. A results-driven marketing strategy that drives business growth begins with an effective website. Notice I used the term effective? Most business owners focus on how good their site looks, and how good it makes them look, not in terms of how Google will register and rank it, which is a mistake. You also must consider how the site looks and functions from a new patient point of view.

The real purpose of a website is to connect with potential new patients and demonstrate to them that you understand their problems. For a weight-loss practice, this means creating a website that provides information, inspiration, and images that will highlight how much you care about these potential new patients and their struggle with being overweight. A website must be designed to meet one business objective, convert new website traffic into actual patient traffic. This is what we call the conversion rate. What do I mean by conversion?

Conversion is the process of driving Internet traffic to your website and then designing it so people will be inspired to call your office to make that first appointment. It sounds simple, but it isn't. You must use the site to connect with potential new patients in a uniquely personal way. Design your website with one goal: Motivate new patients to trust you and call your practice!

Your staff can also impact conversion rates. Train them to work with potential new clients on the phone and make it more likely that calls will turn into appointments. Your team can also be responsible for converting new patients into recurring patients by providing excellent service and care.

A high conversion rate begins with a functional and informative website that speaks directly to the patient. You understand their problems, and your services will help them achieve their goals.

Warning: Developing a new website can be a minefield of expensive mistakes and strategic errors.

Your website development must be managed by someone with a deep understanding of Internet marketing from the aesthetics down to knowing how to code it and get it recognized and ranked by Google. One classic mistake is hiring a team of designers who have only a superficial knowledge of how online marketing works. Big marketing agencies and web designers will suggest a complex website with beautiful graphics. You'll hear phrases like parallax web design, asymmetric grid, dynamic content, split content, micro-interactions, and intuitive interface. These may be cool features, and if your goal is an expensive, flashy website, then go ahead and take this route. But I don't recommend it. These sites are rarely designed with either Google web standards or new patients in mind. They look great but rank extremely low in search results. You won't get seen, and patients will not be engaged.

The second most popular option is the DIY site. It's built by a friend, or a friend of a cousin, or whomever. It's a low-cost option until you realize that it's a pre-packaged, cookie-cutter, and unprofessional. You'll end up with mediocre photos, stolen content, and a hefty monthly fee for updates and maintenance. And, the site still won't register with search engines so it won't get ranked. If you don't show up in search results, you won't get new patients. This is costly, no matter how inexpensive it may seem at first.

Practitioners must keep one goal in mind when designing a website: attracting potential new patients. A fancy site developed by an agency that has interactive menus and customized features distracts the audience. It makes it difficult for people to get the information they are hungry for, even if they find you. DIY sites don't work much better. Amateur sites look unprofessional, and they don't show up in online searches, and patients don't find the information they want most.

What's the solution?

A website constructed and coded to register with Google and other search engine crawlers. And give potential new clients what they want! (1) A modest, straightforward website with useful information, (2) a list of your services, and (3) a sense of who you are so that they will trust you enough to call your office and schedule an appointment. Makes sense, right?

Our data shows that a well designed, straightforward website with informative content, carefully selected keywords, and good quality photos are all that you need. And, of course, it must be coded with search engine algorithms in mind. Combine this kind of site, link it with original social media content, and before long, your practice will rise in search engine results. Your practice will be discovered by new audiences who will visit the site and then call for an appointment. A new website pays off only if it brings in a steady stream of new patient calls and visits every month. That's the right kind of site.

Be Basic

We've been talking about the importance of getting high search engine rankings, and the next chapter discusses the specifics of that. However, before we move ahead, I want to share the basics needed for a compelling, successful website.

We have a secret formula for drawing pre-qualified website traffic, people who are ready to call for an appointment. The first challenge is separating that qualified traffic from "window shoppers" or idle Internet surfers. The specifics of how to do this are covered later on in the book. For now, just understand that our strategy drives only people who are already interested in your services. By following certain rules, you can create a site that converts site visitors into new patient calls to your clinic. So, let's take a look.

The first rule is looking at the language you use. Online content is now how we communicate. How you "speak" to people, in writing, matters a great deal. Imagine for a moment what a potential new patient is going through. How do they feel about the issue of weight loss? What are their concerns, their struggles? Show them, using the right language and the right images, that your practice is the place to call. Our studies show that the more modest, caring, and informative a website is, the more phone calls and conversions the practice experiences. A robust, functional website speaks to the patient's needs and is more successful. So, what does the "right" site look like? It's limited to a few basic but essential pages.

Home Page
Blog

About Us
Services
Contact Us

And, that's it.

If you've ever gotten a website or marketing proposal from an agency, the simplicity of our website can seem underwhelming. But these sites work! A fancy, complex website with too many bells and whistles is hard for potential new patients to navigate. This causes them to be slow to pick up the phone and act on their impulse.

Imagine being overweight and at home. You are quite likely frustrated, embarrassed, or afraid of failing. You decide to do an online search to feel better. There is a spark of motivation to make a change. According to the research, the first thing you'll do is type in "weight loss boston," or something similar. As results flood the screen, sometimes as many as 160 million listings, you pour over the list. What is it you will look for? Any listing for a weight loss service that is nearby and convenient, with positive reviews.

Let's say you click on a listing and jump to a website. If what you find is straightforward information and a sense that someone cares about your struggle, you're going to stay on the site. If there are great patient reviews, a special offer, and a professional approach, you are far more likely to call that doctor. People simply want to know that they are dealing with an experienced professional who is trustworthy and cares about their weight loss problems.

The weight loss market, in particular, is overrun with flashy ads, wild discounts on unproven supplements. Some clinics push invasive and expensive surgical options. Potential new patients won't identify with fake miracles or false promises. They can't afford, nor do they want to undergo drastic surgery. Give them clear information regarding your affordable, practical weight loss solution. Highlight the success your patients have experienced and let them know that you can be trusted. This is the content that makes it easy for a new patient to call.

Imagine being desperate to lose weight, searching for support on the Internet, and in the middle of all of the B.S., you find a listing by a trusted medical doctor, in your neighborhood, who is a real person. Your website lets them know you understand their struggle, that you have helped others.

Give them success stories and excellent reviews written by real people. Show them there is someone who cares. That's how you get the call for an appointment.

Every page on your site can be simple, include useful information, and a phone number or contact form that makes it easy for them to reach out. A results-driven website has practical information, real photos, and shows potential new patients what to expect when they come and see you. These tactics are from marketing 101, principles tried and true for as long as advertising has been around. But, it's marketing 101 applied to online tactics, which is necessary for today's online culture full of scams and information overload.

Flashy websites, animated graphics, complicated medical jargon, fear tactics, false promises, your potential new patients have seen it all. It will be a relief when they find a medical professional that understands their issues and is committed to supporting them on their weight loss journey.

Web Design that Works

Pro Tip: Every page on the website must have a call-to-action. "Call-to-action" is the phrase we use to describe how a visitor to the site is prompted to take action. Do you want the potential new patient to call the clinic? Do you want to present a special offer? Do you want to entice them to submit their contact information? These all require a Call- to-Action banner.

The right call-to-action is one that accomplishes the business goal.

I will cover in a bit the elements that go into designing a call-to-action. But, for now, just understand that for a weight loss physician two things are critical. First, we recommend putting a banner or header with your phone number on every single page. Position it in the top-right corner or the middle-right hand side. Research shows that when people see a page, their eyes automatically drift to the right. Since we read left to right, this makes perfect sense. Go online and look where Google places its ads.

A second recommendation is adding a link to a form beneath the phone number. This is where potential new clients will sign up for your customized newsletter, packed with useful information and fun topics. You can also include an incentive that will inspire them to provide a phone number and email address. Staying in touch is an excellent way for you to guide them into becoming new patients over time.

With the right tactics, people will come to your website pre-qualified from targeted social media links. They will have expressed an interest in the services your clinic provides, even if they aren't ready to commit. And, that's OK. Add them to the list and stay in touch. When they're ready, you'll be the first one they call.

Outside of the Call to Action, feel free to modify the website framework and layout any way that makes sense. Add more features, like an events page where you can announce upcoming special offers or a free nutritious cooking seminar. Just make sure the events page can be easily updated. Include a Recent News page where you can publish press releases (that you write) about your practice, or new blog posts. Apply to win a community health award or get quoted in a health publication. Create a "Loser of the Month" corner featuring a patient who is making significant progress. These are all things you can promote as news items on your site. Make it fun, informative, and useful, and soon you will be connecting with hundreds of potential new patients. Just remember that a basic layout is always better-the simpler the page, the better your results.

Pro Tip: Do not confuse "basic layout" with poor design. You want the website to look professional. It's a reflection of your medical expertise and your desire to solve your patient's weight loss problems. We've found that a clean, straightforward design works best. Stay away from flashy graphics, tons of links, phony stock photos, or interactive features; they break down anyway! Don't distract website visitors from your primary goal; getting them to call your office for an appointment. And, don't build a DIY site that looks cookie-cutter generic or cheap. You may save a little money in the short term, but it won't bring you any new patients in the long run. Present yourself as a local weight loss expert who provides a vital health service and is community-minded.

My marketing strategies are metrics-driven. We issue monthly call reports to our clients, leaving no doubt that websites with "less" lead to more, as in more phone calls and more new patients.

One last word about website design. If you've already invested in branding and a logo that represents your business, by all means, use it. If you haven't, you can do this in-house. There are color palette tools online that will allow you to select core color preferences and receive a suggested palette of visually appealing, complementary colors that designers can use. One example is Colour Lovers (http://www.colourlovers.com). Another option is Color Combos (http://www.colorcombos.com). These sites are easy to use and will help you sort through the initial design decisions and pass them on to your web designer.

Now, let's break down the pages that are necessary for a successful website.

A Home Page with Heart

Your HOME page shouldn't be about you, at least not at first. The home page is about your new patient. It must let them know that you understand their needs when it comes to weight loss. We all know first impressions are vitally important. The first rule of a great home page is resisting the urge to make it all about you; it's about your new patients.

When you attend an event and meet someone new, how do you feel when all they do is talk about themselves? You never get a word in. It's annoying and makes you want to tune out. Websites that are all about YOU are the same. When someone gets to your HOME page if it's full of boasts and language about how great your practice is, but nothing that speaks to their issues, they'll exit quickly. You're cheating potential new patients out of a two-way conversation and exchange of information.

However, if your content shows compassion and connects with them on a personal level, it will draw them in. Let website visitors know that you understand their problems with weight loss and show them you care enough to share practical information and inspiring stories. It's fine to give a summary of your practice. Your focus needs to be on how you can help them tackle the issue they are attempting to address. You're going to make it possible for them to lose weight and achieve their long term health goals! Later, on other pages, you can highlight your services and bio.

Remember, online marketing, appropriately done, drives qualified traffic to your website. The traffic consists of people already searching for your weight loss services. They don't have to be "sold." However, they do need to see that you are (1) available locally, (2) that you understand what they're going through, and (3) you are a practitioner that can be trusted.

By the time they land on your site, people have already wandered through a vast desert of listings. They've seen the pushy sales tactics, and they've seen fake pictures and false results. When they discover that you are a real physician focused on their needs, who has gotten results for others, it will be like a breath of fresh air. You'll earn their attention, but you'll also win their trust. And that's what makes the phone ring.

In terms of graphic design, as we've said before, less is more. However, make it appealing with branded colors, and include (briefly) information about your practice and services. The design should allow for easy navigation by being well organized. And, don't forget the sidebars, the call-to-action banners on every page. Always be inviting visitors to call for an appointment or fill out a contact form.

One additional home page rule, it must feature your blog prominently! Featuring a blog is so vitally important, I can't overstate it enough. There are several ways to do it in terms of placement, and ultimately, it's up to you and your web designer. However, it must be thoughtful. Blog posts should be placed where they are easy to find. Here's why; For one thing, a successful online marketing strategy involves distributing excerpts from blog posts on social sites. These summaries go out to thousands of people with links that will draw them to your website. Once they visit, they'll explore it and find out more about you.

Second, blog posts contain keywords, images, and video. If published on your site and appropriately indexed, the search engines will use this data to rank your website. Some technical know-how is required to do this correctly, but for now, I am just trying to stress how important it is to include blogs on your home page and keep them updated.

Video is another necessary component of a good home page.

Studies have shown a 30% increase in conversions when a visitor watches a video on your homepage. This video can be you, a staff member, or, better yet, patients sharing positive feedback. It bears repeating that research shows a 30% increase in the number of people who go from being a website visitor to a new patient when you include video. Incorporate a short (somewhere between 90 seconds and 2 minutes) video on your homepage, and you'll start to see results.

Make your content clear, relevant, thoughtful, and ORIGINAL!

Copy on your home page should include only three things:

1.) The benefits a patient will experience when working with your practice. Not your services or "features," but real results. How will their lives improve? Give them a vision of what their life will be like if they work with you. Show them how their lives will change for the better when they lose weight.

2.) New useful information about topics they are interested in, including weight loss. Make this content available on blogs with small excerpts links, and that will entice them to click through and visit your website. Include just enough to make them want to explore your site and read more.

3.) A strong call-to-action. A motivational message to act is included on every page. Inspire them, give them hope. Let them know your practice is one that will help solve their issues with weight loss. Make the action clear and straightforward. Invite them to take that next step. Encourage them to call you for a consultation or to fill out the contact form. Use exclusive offers, informative reports, or a fun quiz or checklist. Make it engaging and inspiring.

These three features are critical to the success of any weight loss website. It can be challenging to get this exactly right, which is why we manage the writing and website design process for our clients. We can guarantee that the web content is audience-focused and published on every relevant platform for maximum effect. Otherwise, your website is just an expensive billboard that no one but you will see. I don't mean to sound harsh, but I hate to see practitioners spend money on websites that fail to bring in new business.

Blogging for Business Success

Your blog is one of the most vital aspects of your marketing plan and your website. It provides two things critical to online success.

First, a well-written blog post draws current and prospective patients to your website, where they will find new and relevant content that is important to them. There are so many topics to write about; health, nutrition, exercise, meditation, the psychology of overeating. There is no end to the ideas that new patients might find interesting, informative, and inspiring.

Second, sharing recent news and articles from other expert sources in the field and linking their content with yours, demonstrates to Google that you are a respected member of the industry. Share news and add your expert commentary. Readers will appreciate hearing about what you think and associate you with other experts. This inspires trust.

There is a third approach we use, and it's a concept that few practices take advantage of, sharing local news. By including information and events from the community, you demonstrate that you are a valuable part of that community. It doesn't have to be about weight loss, and in fact, it shouldn't be! You are an active member of a city, town, and neighborhood. Show these new patients that you are a community-minded practitioner. Share news about a local 5k run, or a fundraiser. Give potential new patients a quick guide to a local food festival. Sponsor a community parade. Write a few paragraphs about a local topic and include links to where they can find details online.

At first, this might sound strange. As a medical practitioner, perhaps you think you should project a serious demeanor 100% of the time. Not true! People, especially potential new patients, will love to discover that you are accessible and real. You might be surprised at how popular this type of content is. By focusing not on weight loss all the time, but also community news, you build credibility. Become that practitioner who lives, works, and cares about the local community, and the phone will ring with new patient appointments. It also earns you points with Google because they love showing their users local content.

Pro Tip: Blogs play an essential role in search engine rankings. If set up correctly, blog posts will register with the search engine crawlers. They're tasked with scraping the Internet every four hours to new, relevant content. Keywords are critical also, but they are only one part of the equation. The most valuable thing is to publish new content consistently, blogs that are 100% original. Search engine crawlers love fresh, original articles, and blog posts. This gets Google to pay attention and rank your site higher. Crawlers come by every four hours like clockwork. If a few weeks go by and they don't find anything new from you, your website will sink like a stone in the rankings.

As a medical practitioner, it's natural to share your ideas in your area of expertise, such as health, wellness, and weight loss. Keywords will probably show up naturally. If you combine this expertise with news and information about the local community, it's a double punch. You'll score higher. Google and other search engines must "see" your practice as a valuable part of your city, town, and neighborhood. This gives your weight loss practice an incredible advantage in terms of business growth.

Acting local and keeping up with content creation isn't complicated, although it can be a challenge to understand and implement at first. Big marketing agencies would love you to believe that it's a mystery that only they can solve. A huge task that only they can accomplish. They'll use terms like "keyword density," "latent search algorithms," and other fancy technical words. If you hear these phrases in a marketing pitch, run! It isn't that hard! Just write about what you know, share expert information, and add local items of interest. In this way, you will keep people reading and engaged with your practice.

Time to Write

Over the years, we've learned a great deal about working with medical practitioners. Consistent blogging is crucial but also time-consuming. When you are busy running a thriving practice, the focus is converting calls into patients and treating them. Writing an 800-word blog post twice a week can be quite a hurdle, whether you are a good writer or not. And, aside from the content, these blog posts must be constructed in a way that the search engines will register it as relevant to search results.

That's why I provide professional writing services for my clients. We craft the content because we understand what works and how busy you are. We've assembled a team of writers who are experts in many different industries and your local community. We have the expertise to know how the search engines work and what kind of content gets picked up. The unbeatable combination of high-quality writing and technical know-how results in better rankings and more qualified traffic. We hire expert writers, and we pay them well, so your content is always original and compelling. This quality of writing is what puts our clients on the map and draws new patients into their practice.

There is data to support the idea that a well-written, well-placed blog generates new business. That's why we handle this for our clients. They receive two or three high-quality posts a week, while they continue to see and treat the new patients that come in. Why not manage a growing weight-loss practice, rather than writing your time away?

About Us Page

This is the website page that most practitioners, marketers, and web designers get terribly wrong.

The About Us page is not the place to brag. It's not an opportunity to list your many medical degrees, certifications, or push your status as a doctor. Surprisingly, the About Us page is not where you highlight your staff or publish a long list of services. The purpose of this page is to express the commitment you make to solving the problems your new patient has. Answer their questions. Speak about their concerns. Show them how you will help them lose weight, and provide case studies of patients who have. How is your practice unique and different? Let them know.

In marketing circles, this is called the USP, your Unique Selling Proposition. Why do your current patients like working with you? This information, presented with integrity, simplicity, and proof, is how good marketing works! Use the About Us page to explain why you are different, trustworthy, and a practitioner that helps the patient achieve results. They'll choose to visit you over any other weight loss center they find online, guaranteed.

The only thing a prospective new patient REALLY wants to know is how you will change their life. They want to hear a story about how you supported someone on their weight loss journey. Distinguish yourself as being entirely different from other weight loss practices, and earn their trust. Let them know how committed you are to changing their life for the better. Inspire them, motivate them, and give them a reason to call your practice for an appointment. This is how to build a results-driven About Us page.

Honestly, your prospects could care less about your many degrees, titles, or status in the medical community. We're sorry to tell you this, but the only thing a potential new patient wants to know is if you can solve their problem in a professional manner. Somewhere on your site, you can list your medical degrees, expertise, or accomplishments. Use the About Us page to show new patients how they will succeed, and you will succeed in earning their trust.

Pro Tip: Always spend more time talking about the patient than your practice. How will they benefit from working with you? This is one of the most important tips I can offer. It sets your practice apart from competitors. Most struggling medical practices we hear from are not growing because they fail to consider the potential new patient's point of view. Take some time to be thoughtful about how your services are different, and how you can communicate that to a new person. By doing so, you will gain a very healthy competitive edge.

Services Page

Likely, the services page isn't the first thing potential customers see on your website. Perhaps they came in through blog posts, or Google searches brought them to your home page. Either way, they want to know more about you—but that doesn't necessarily mean they already have a good idea of what you do. Sure, some visitors have already read your home page and FAQs, but others came in via social media or a blog post and haven't read anything else. They chose to click on the services page because they want to find out more.

Before asking people to dig into the details, give them a top-level view of what you do and the unique value you offer (a.k.a. your elevator pitch). This opens the door for further conversation and establishes the context they'll use to interpret the rest of the information they read. It may be all they read if they're just beginning to check you out. Make sure to use the main keyword (the one that appears in the page title) to optimize the page for search engines. While some people will read this section, others won't, and SEO is one of its vital functions.

Finally, focus on the overall benefits a patient gains from doing business with you, rather than detailing individual services. Aim for 100-150 words, and keep the needs and pain points of your ideal customer in mind. Finish it out with 1-2 sentences demonstrating what qualifies you to provide these services. You'll have other pages devoted to all of your qualifications; here, reinforce your claims with something specific, like an award, certification, or number of years of experience and why that benefits the customer.

Contact Us

The Contact Us page is straightforward. Provide your email address, your office address, your phone number, and a map. That's it. If you feel it's necessary, you can punch it up with a more persuasive call-to-action, but for the most part, Contact Us means precisely that.

Some marketers suggest not including your email. As the theory goes, this forces people to call you instead. Then you have a chance to "sell" them, but this is a mistake, in my opinion. Anyone not ready to call you, won't. But, they might email you for more information, which allows you to stay in touch.

Clean, easy-to-read, and act upon, that's what a Contact Us page is all about. Adding a contact form for a visitor to fill out is excellent, but if you do so, be sure that you have a follow-up system. The only way to convert these leads is to respond with quick and meaningful messages.

Call-to-Action

By now, you understand basically what a call-to-action is. And, you remember from an earlier chapter that one should be placed strategically on every page. But, what makes a compelling call-to-action message? How can you craft one that triggers a web visitor to take action?

The primary goal of the call-to-action is to encourage potential new patients to call your office. Whether they seek information or to schedule a consultation, a call-to-action helps them push the button. Of course, getting people to take action is tricky. There will always be a percentage of people who are not quite ready to call. It can be a timing issue (maybe it's late at night, and they know you won't be open), or they are hesitant to take that first step to lose weight. There are ways to draw them in closer and keep the lines of communication open. One way is to collect their information and stay in touch until they are ready.

Pro Tip: What I am about to mention may sound crazy, but double-check that your phone system is working correctly. Is the voicemail set up with a warm, welcoming message? If a call comes in and it is not during business hours, you still have an opportunity to make an excellent first impression. Your voicemail can be a quick introduction to your practice, and an invitation to leave a phone number and email address. Promise a timely return message.

During business hours, the staff must be trained to answer the phone within one or two rings. Make sure those who answer the phones announce the name of the practice clearly in a warm, friendly tone. Then, have them ask the caller how they can help. Train your staff to listen carefully and with empathy. There is nothing worse than working endless hours to get new patients to call a practice, only to discover that no one is answering the phone, or the staff is rude to new patients.

There is no better way to waste a marketing investment than to blow it during this last step. Your staff must be made to understand that new patient calls are the lifeblood of a thriving practice. Let them know it has cost a significant amount to bring the calls in, and that every caller is essential. Please, don't be the practice that doesn't treat callers with respect.

The Special Offer

Your call-to-action banner must be concise, clear, and trustworthy. People resist giving up their contact information. They are VERY aware that giving out this information puts them at risk of receiving SPAM emails. Either they've heard about scams, or they've been a victim. For many good reasons, people hesitate to submit their contact information. Make it worth their while. Offer a special incentive, such as a comprehensive study, a discount code, or a special offer. Make a promise that you won't sell their data or use it for nefarious purposes and then KEEP THAT PROMISE.

In our many years of marketing success, we've found that providing an informative report works well. Provide a simple, clear offer of a white paper, or an article that will appeal to someone looking to lose weight.

One example might be, "The 3 Myths About Exercise and Weight Loss," or "Five Easy Ways To Eat Less." This free report must be specific to your practice. The more targeted the examples are, the more likely it is that they will sign up and give you their information. You can make the report even more targeted by creating messaging that is local. For example: "3 Things to Learn About Medical Weight Loss in Garden City." Again, the report must be strong enough to motivate someone to give up their contact information.

Even if they are ready to call, a compelling offer might lead them to sign up AND call, which is a big win.

Once a potential new patient submits an email address and requests the report, you must be ready. Have the report and follow-up communications lined up so you can commit to timely and meaningful responses. There are ways to automate this process, while still making it warm and personal, which is essential. (We'll cover setting up convenient, automated follow-up messages later in this guide).

Follow-up content is critical, so this is another service we provide to clients. We write reports with proper keyword phrases and geolocation indicators and place this content strategically on their website (with their approval, of course). Our reports take a "consumer advocacy" approach, which means the material is written from the consumer's point of view, not the provider's. In other words, these reports are not ads disguised as information; they are genuinely informative. Only this kind of content is enticing enough to earn the trust of new patients.

If you follow these steps, those who sign up with their email address and phone number become "warm" leads. A warm lead is receptive to your communications and has some familiarity with your business. These leads are much easier to convert into new patients. By submitting their information, they are demonstrating an interest in your services. The hard part is over, getting their attention and leading them into signing up. However, the work is far from over.

Once they join your list, you must ACT FAST! Warm leads tend to cool off quickly. If you don't communicate right away with relevant, exciting content, you'll lose them. The longer you wait, the harder it is to convert them to a new patient. That's why we offer our clients automated follow-up systems with pre-written content loaded and ready to go.

You must have a stable, reliable automated system of follow-up. If you don't, all the work you've done to get these warm leads might be wasted. There are plenty of options. You can automate a recorded phone message that goes straight to their voicemail within five minutes of their submission. Welcome them to your practice and let them know you are available to answer any questions. Very few practices do this, and it will set you apart. You can also record a friendly, personal message letting them know you have a special offer and to be on the lookout for it. Send this within 5 minutes of receiving the contact form, and you'll be viewed as a professional and caring service. These potential new patients will be more open to hearing from you, which is the very definition of a warm lead.

Don't wait "until you have time" to follow up. Days turn into weeks, and then months. By then, these potential new patients will have moved on, wasting all of your marketing efforts.

Tools of the Trade

There are several tools available to automate follow-up campaigns. Systems like Aweber, Constant Contact, or Infusionsoft, are just a few of the packages on the market. Be careful. Most medical practitioners we work with don't have the time, or desire, to write and schedule all of that content. Some of these systems come with features that can help, like pre-written email templates, for example. While these tools are better than doing nothing, they aren't foolproof. Canned content that is not original to you doesn't always bring results. If you do go this route, task someone with managing the process with both technical expertise and marketing experience. Place a call-to-action on every page, send timely, relevant information, and always project an image of a local, professional practitioner who cares. Show them you are ready to help them achieve their weight loss goals.

Automated tools are a viable in-house option, but make sure this entire call-to-action and follow up process is being implemented WITH all of the other recommendations in this book. As a stand-alone effort, it's not enough. Now, let's move on to the core marketing issue, getting your website seen by tens of thousands of new viewers, rather than ten, which is far more common.

Get FREE Content That Will Help You Get More New Patient Calls And Leads From Your Website Here: http://website-weight-loss.com

Chapter 4: Keying Into Words That Work

Finding the Right Keywords to Bring In New Patients

You can launch one of the best-looking websites in your industry and market, but who's seeing it? Sadly, in most cases, you are the only one paying attention. Expensive sites are often merely vanity projects. I apologize if this sounds harsh, but it's a truth I feel obligated to share. A website without an underlying business objective built to achieve Google rankings is just an expensive billboard on a lonely road with no traffic.

Hundreds of businesses and practices fall into this trap. They tell me that having a significant online presence isn't essential for their business. Then, in the next breath, I hear that they've spent tens of thousands of dollars to launch a new website without seeing an increase in new patient traffic. Far too many businesses waste valuable resources on sites that don't have a strategic marketing objective! If being seen online isn't essential for the growth of the practice, why are they spending so much time, energy, and capital on a site and one-off SEO services? Especially when those efforts fail to bring in new patients.

Every medical weight loss practice would benefit from a strategic online marketing plan and website that drives new, qualified patients to their clinic. But, without ranking for strategic keywords, new patients won't find you. Remember the statistics we highlighted in chapter two. Ninety-seven percent of people looking for services research online before making any decisions. Here's another critical statistic: Of the 97% who research services online, 71% click only on listings included in the first page of results. That means page two won't do. If you are not showing up on page one for key phrases and a geographic location, you are losing an incredibly deep pool of potential new patients.

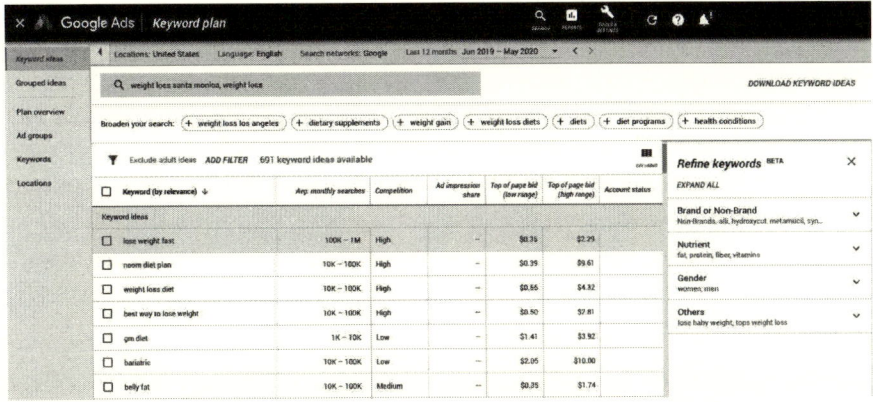

Keywords are the Key to Success

There is a positive chain reaction when you publish a website, distribute effective content with links, and list your business correctly with Google and local directories. These are just a few of the necessary items I have included on your online marketing TO-DO list. Building a simple, useful website that serves as a marketing hub is a priority. It must be organized well, coded for Google and search engines, and have carefully selected keyword phrases embedded in the text. So, how do you choose what keywords to use? Let's find out.

Search engines rank your site by sending crawlers to scrape your content and look for relevant search data, among other criteria. In this highly competitive cyber world, Google is King. Search engine crawlers work 24/7 seeking to identify sites and content most relevant to the people using the tool. These bots are hungry for content that is fresh and new, and popular. It's their sole mission to continually find and rank content, and evaluate how valuable it is to their users. If your site never has new content or relevant keywords, you are a nobody as far as the search engines are concerned.

Explaining how this works in detail, requires a highly technical conversation that most practitioners would rather not have. However, without a basic understanding of keywords and how they are used to rank in search results, you can't hire the right marketing team, a marketing con artist could take advantage of you. Real marketing success results in a thriving, profitable practice with new patients calling every day. This requires an in-depth knowledge of keyword use.

Keywords are the words (either one word or multiple words in a phrase) that users type into the Google search bar. A person searching for help with weight loss might type in a phrase such as "weight loss center near me" or 'weight loss South Dakota." This is called a long-tail keyword phrase. When they enter the words into a search box, it becomes a "keyword phrase." The phrase they use determines which sites or directories will be delivered in their results. Web crawlers assess the most relevant information on the Internet based on the words people use most often to search. The returns they see are what Google and other engines consider the best match based on the keywords they type in. Finding keywords that will work to your advantage is both an art and a science. It's critical to figure out which keywords Google will recognize as relevant to its users, using analytics (science) and human nature (art).

Getting your content and website to show up on the first page of search results is the goal and the challenge. The complexity of Google algorithms and the determination of excellent keyword selection are two reasons businesses seek our help to manage their online marketing. Not having a handle on effective keywords is the main reason many DIY marketing efforts fail.

During the onboarding process with new clients, we typically uncover two keyword selection failures. First, they misunderstand how keywords work. Practitioners are proud to show us how they rank number one for their business name. Not to be discouraging, but this is hardly a success. Think about it logically. A potential new patient that has never heard of you won't be able to use your business name when searching! Ranking for your business name won't help new patients find you.

Marketing teams claim big wins because they've gotten you to rank for your business name, but the way Google is set up, your website under your corporate name is likely to show up anyway. Anyone searching from an I.P. address within 25 miles of your location will probably see you somewhere on the first few pages, no matter what. It's just not that hard to get listed under your practice name. However, new patients searching online can't search using your business name as the keyword phrase, because they don't know who you are yet! Is this a big deal? Remember that 97% of the people looking for your services are doing so online. However, they are not using your business name to conduct their search. When results fill up their screen, you won't be on the list.

Don't let a marketing agency fool you into thinking they've done a terrific job if a search using your practice name brings up your listing. If the goal is to use the Internet to get new patients (and why wouldn't it be?), you need to walk in the shoes of someone looking for your services and use the same words they use. What keywords are they using to conduct their online search? Determining that is what will lead to new patient traffic. What services do your potential new patients look for? How do they phrase it? Use those keyword phrases strategically on your site, in your blogs, and in directory listings. Soon, you'll start seeing results.

It takes expertise and effort to find keyword phrases that work, but it is the only way to develop an effective marketing SEO strategy. People who are intensely searching for "weight loss doctor," or "ways to lose weight," these are the people you want to find you.

The only successful marketing plan is one that brings new patients into your practice. Accomplish this by ranking for specific keywords related to the problems people have, the issues that you solve. It's OK to rank for your business name, but ranking for the core services that people are looking for, and that you provide, is what leads to business growth.

The second common mistake are keyword selections based on sophisticated medical terms, words that only medical professionals understand. These are not the words or phrases that ordinary people use when they search online. A keyword phrase like "laparoscopic adjustable banding," may tell another practitioner about a service, but the average person won't use that phrase to search for weight loss help.

Remember, potential new patients won't find you by using your name, medically dense phrases, or scientific jargon. If those are the keywords in your content, your site probably will not end up in the search results that matter.

Tracking the Data

Pro Tip: Google tracks and offers data about what phrases people are using in their searches. I'm sure you've heard the word analytics. You can use these tools to research trending topics as well as the most popular search phrases for an industry or subject. While many analytic tools are free to use, deciphering the data and translating it into business growth is more complicated. It may require professional help.

One mistake I see a lot are marketing amateurs or business owners looking at the analytics and selecting a keyword phrase because millions of people use that phrase in searches. They think it's the best choice because it's popular. This is a mistake. When too many people are using a generic phrase like "weight loss," the competition to show up and rank for that phrase is fierce. Companies that have deep pockets pay dearly to show up for those highly competitive phrases. You'll be playing catch-up for a very long time and spend a lot of money. My analytics team tracks every move Google makes and assesses search trends in industries and specific markets. We identify unique keyword phrases that are not as broad or too generic. Our mission to uncover less obvious but still commonly used keywords. We know how to use language that ordinary people use, thereby creating a perfect match between potential new patients and your weight loss practice. We understand Google's search rules and how people behave online, and we help you and your new weight loss patient find each other.

The most important thing to remember in keyword selection is this: you must consider keywords from the patient's perspective. You can't assume what search terms they might use. You can't be concerned about how you look to other practitioners, and you shouldn't use complicated medical terms. Resist the urge to use status-seeking phrases or generic words that are too broad, and therefore too competitive.

If you find after reading this that your keywords selections are all wrong, don't be discouraged. It's a common problem. When promoting my business, I have to be strategic, just like you do. If I end up using a phrase that you aren't familiar with, such as "metrics of online marketing," my business doesn't get traffic. We run analytics on our content all the time, tweaking keywords so that new clients like you will find us. A significant benefit to hiring a consulting group like ours is that we understand how to use keywords to achieve your number one goal, bringing new weight loss patients into your practice.

Most major pitfalls regarding keyword phrases involve the same root problem, a lack of knowledge about how search engine algorithms and strategic keywords interact. In this case, knowledge is power. Determine which search phrases are trending in medical weight loss, use keywords that will register in that niche, and you will get new traffic.

Tools of the Trade

There is software that serves a diagnostic tool, helping determine keywords that will generate traffic and improve rankings. If you want to know my thoughts on the effectiveness of buying and using one of these tools, here it is. They can be useful down the road after you've already launched a full marketing program. But, when it comes to your initial launch, no one knows your practice or the type of new patient you are looking for, better than you do. Surely you know your business better than a piece of software.

The choice of language involves human emotion and interaction. You can intuit the words that will appeal to a person who is overweight, discouraged, and determined to change. Can software make non-generic word choices that will speak to them with empathy and concern for their well being? I think not. Remember, it's ordinary people using ordinary language through Google, Bing, or other search engines. When you launch, use appealing text and practical keyword selections.

Here's a pro tip. Ask a current patient or a friend to explain your practice to you and listen carefully. Doing informal research can help you make good keyword choices. I'm willing to bet that if you interview people you know, you'll hear plain words that describe a problem that people have, rather than sophisticated descriptions. Whatever phrases a current patient has used, other new patients are likely using those same phrases. Determine what the average person is typing into the search box, and you're halfway there.

Here's another way to select keywords. Give a 30-second description to a person that doesn't know anything about your practice or weight loss. Then, ask them to turn and describe it to someone else. Can they do it quickly? What words do they remember and repeat? This is another way to discover new keywords and phrases that will improve your ranking and bring more qualified traffic to your site.

Keywords are not something you need to get 100% perfect right away. That's why Google Analytics is a useful tool. Select a series of keywords, launch your site and online marketing campaigns, and assess how they perform over time. Three months is usually long enough to determine how well your keywords are performing. If the traffic to your site isn't increasing or your conversions from calls to new patients aren't high enough, you can modify, refine, or switch out a few keyword phrases and try again. There is no need to overthink this aspect of marketing. Later on, as you begin to have some success, you can try using one of the tools available to refine your keyword selection.

Searches related to weight loss doctors

Q weight loss doctors **near me**

Q weight loss doctors **in**

Q weight loss doctors **in**

Q weight loss doctors **nj**

Q **hormone** weight loss **doctor**

Q weight loss **clinic**

Q weight loss **specialist**

Q **bariatric physician**

1 2 3 4 5 6 7 8 9 10   Next

Another way my team analyzes keyword selection even further is by using Google's "Related Searches" tool. By researching this category, you'll find ideas for additional and similar phrases people are using to search for help with weight loss. This tool gives you insight directly from Google about trending terms people are using, and new phrases you might not have thought of before.

Another important weapon in your keyword arsenal is the Google Keyword Tool (GKT for short). While the "Related Searches" tool offers suggestions, GKT is just data. This tool will tell you the number of returns for specific keywords and how many people per month use these phrases. The data is drawn from searches all across the United States, so you have to make an educated guess about what keywords will work in your geographic location. An in-depth understanding of these tools is another key benefit we offer our clients. To explain it further, let's use these examples, "weight loss" and "losing weight."

Keyword (by relevance) ↓	Avg. monthly searches	Competition	Ad impression share	Top of page bid (low range)	Top of page bid (high range)	Account status
lose weight fast	100K – 1M	High	–	$0.35	$2.29	
noom diet plan	10K – 100K	High	–	$0.39	$9.61	
weight loss diet	10K – 100K	High	–	$0.55	$4.32	
best way to lose weight	10K – 100K	High	–	$0.50	$7.81	
gm diet	1K – 10K	Low	–	$1.41	$3.92	
bariatric	10K – 100K	Low	–	$2.05	$10.00	
belly fat	10K – 100K	Medium	–	$0.35	$1.74	

Google Keyword Planner Tool

You'll notice in the screenshot above that "weight loss" shows up more often than "losing weight" in nationwide results. You can assume that in your local area, the numbers in the GKT might be similar, but it's not an exact science. There haven't been tools developed yet that can pinpoint analytics on local searches. The current systems aren't capable of tracking data regarding the popularity of locally trending keywords. You have to assume that the national numbers will more or less apply reasonably well to local searches in your area.

So, to gain a better idea of how many local searches there are compared to national numbers, here is a rough calculation. Look at the data from the last census and the numbers in your geographic location. Divide the population data in your area by the total U.S. population. This results in a rough estimate of the fraction your area represents of the total population. Multiply that by the number of "searches" for a keyword, and you can estimate the number of searches happening for a keyword in your area.

Here's a specific example: Let's say you live in a city with eight million people (i.e., New York City). The U.S. counted 300 million people in the last census. So, NYC has 8/300th of the total population. Now, we see that "weight loss," returns 135k hits per month. From this, we can assume your locale gets about 3,600 searches per month on that keyword. It's not exact, but it's a pretty good guess.

As I mentioned before, a higher number is NOT necessarily better. Sometimes, a keyword phrase shows that several million people are searching with that phrase. When people see that 7 million people search using "weight loss," they get excited, imagining that this will be the size of their potential new audience. Sadly, this isn't the case. What it means is that the phrase is highly competitive. Ranking with hugely popular keyword combinations takes an incredible amount of work and considerable financial investment. You have to work harder and wait longer to show up. We find it's more efficient to determine popular keyword phrases, but where there's still room to rank. We call this niche marketing. Niche phrases bring in more than enough new patient traffic to build a busy, profitable practice, or several if that's your goal.

We work on behalf of our clients to ensure that they dominate their market using niche keyword phrases. We test for phrases that are commonly used, but not so competitive that you can't end up on page one. This is how you connect with new audiences and find new patients.

Another common pitfall is using neat, "catchy," names, or phrases in your URL. Gimmicks seem like "attention getters." The idea that a catchy URL that will help you to stand out is a myth. Gimmicky words in a URL mean nothing to Google. Search engine crawlers troll the Internet night and day, collecting data so that they will be ready to return results relevant to their users. These crawlers do not recognize or care about gimmicky words. If you want an excellent ranking that will change your business, create a URL that is sensible and indicates what service you provide. That's what will get Google's attention. Make it keyword-rich and Google friendly.

Here's an example; Let's say you open a weight loss clinic in Dayton, Ohio. You decide the primary keyword phrase should be "Weight Loss City State", a good choice because a potential new patient might use it. It should also become your URL. So, "WeightLossCitySt.com" is an excellent choice. This might give your practice a tremendous boost because crawlers can recognize it and get information from it. Both your primary service and location are in your URL.

We understand that WeightLossCitySt is not "sexy" or memorable so here is another

Pro-Tip: Your keyword-rich URL does not have to be the business URL you give your clients. They can be different! You can choose the URL people will see and use, and an underlying URL that is keyword-rich. Print your catchy website name on your business cards, put it in your emails, publish it on your marketing materials. Then, ask your web manager to redirect your catchy URL to the primary, keyword-rich URL. Maybe you like the sound of "amazingloss.com." But, that phrase means nothing to Google. So, select a Google-friendly URL, and redirect all traffic from "amazingloss. com" to "WeightLossCitySt.com." This way, you reap the benefits of having a keyword-rich URL, but you can also have your memorable URL.

A keyword-based URL can powerfully influence your Google search rankings. We'll talk about other strategies we use to push your practice to the top.

Be advised: the best and often safest URL for your business website is often your brand name WITHOUT any keywords in the URL. The choice that you make in the domain name determines the best strategy. The choice regarding how keywords are used with domain names often varies based on the current Google algorithm.

Find Your Niche

In general, "Niche" relates to products, services, or interests that appeal to a small, specialized section of the population. But, the phrase is used differently in the world of Internet marketing. Also known as "niching" it's the practice of focusing marketing on a single service.

Jamming a URL with multiple services or locations might be possible in a less competitive geographic area, where no one is competing to get into search results. But, finding a market like this is rare. Most of the U.S. has weight loss clinics, supplements, or centers where companies or vying for business. To be competitive, select a niche service to focus on in your keywords, practice descriptions, content and location. Include one service and one geographic location, and you'll turn "niche marketing," into an advantage. Narrowing the focus in your doesn't mean you can't offer a variety of services and "cross-sell" additional services once a person becomes a patient. But, to launch the initial marketing strategy and get new people in the door, you have to commit to a single "niche" service and location as your initial primary strategy. Of course, you can open as many clinics as you wish. Each clinic, however, must be marketed as a separate entity.

We specialize in weight loss because there is such a big demand for that health service.

Of course, if you have extensive medical expertise and training, you treat many health conditions. It can feel limiting to marketing your practice based on one service. You want patients to know all that you are capable of. However, trying to launch and rank online with a list of services or multiple locations doesn't work. Google crawlers find this confusing, and you won't get ranked. If you don't get ranked, your practice won't show up in search results, and new people won't find you. This is a vicious cycle because a lack of click-throughs on your listing also tells Google you are not important.

It can be challenging to become publicly identified as practicing one service. To determine what service to select, I ask several key questions. I might ask you where most of your current revenue comes from, or inquire about the health problems you see occurring most often. What health issues are you good at addressing? We also discuss patient interest. As a doctor, maybe there is an area of expertise that you have, but few people need the service. Deciding which service to list for should also relate to where the most revenue comes from. Weight loss is a sought after service that leads to recurring patient visits. That's why we recommend practitioners focus on this to build a profitable practice. There has to be a thoughtful balance between your expertise, the kind of work you find satisfying, and offering the services that are in demand. This is the key to profitability and building a business you enjoy.

Another thing I ask clients to look at with me is the "cost per patient." Does practicing this service require more extended visits with patients, or can you see many patients per day? Will appointments be recurring or one and done?

As a medical practitioner having this core business and profitability conversation is crucial. Without profitability, you won't have a sustainable practice. This is one reason we recommend weight loss practices. Medical doctors are concerned about patient health, but they also need to be profitable. Why not solve one of the biggest health challenges facing people today and improve patient's lives? You can do that and be profitable with our marketing and business model.

In terms of marketing, what it comes down to is this: To dominate in online searches and be found by potential new patients, you have to focus on one service. Find a service that, if 95% of your business came from providing it, you would be satisfied, and the practice would be profitable. Keyword selection and deciding the service you will rank for is critical to your success.

Start with one goal: a profitable practice that provides one service, a niche that you can absolutely dominate in, in your market. Use a keyword-rich URL and the right keywords, and become the most prominent practitioner online in your market. Once you do this, calls from new patients are practically guaranteed. This is a proven strategy that works.

Titles and Tags

Once keywords have been identified and integrated into a URL, make sure those keyword phrases are in the "title tag" on your website. The title tag must ALWAYS start with the keywords, and be followed by the location. You can end with the business name, just don't lead with the practice name. Not to worry, your practice name will still be all over your website, and patients will see it. However, to get ranked in search results, the keywords have to be embedded in the title tag, and placed first! Then you can use the business name throughout the text on the site.

Pro Tip: Don't overdo it! Google wants to provide value to its searchers. Their algorithms are designed to look for real content, written and published by real people, running real businesses. Their goal is to provide value to their searching customers. Like any business, Google needs to keep its customers happy by giving them a good user experience as they search. They DO NOT LIKE companies that use SPAM, or tools that spew out keywords nonstop. Jamming a site with unreadable text overrun with keywords is frowned upon. There's even a keywords-themed joke in the Search Engine Optimization (SEO) world about this:

Q: How many Search Engine experts does it take to change a light bulb?
A: Twelve! Light. Bulb. Lamp. Fluorescent. Incandescent. LED. Flashlight. Lights. Bulbs. Lamps. Bulbs R Us. Lights R Us.

While the joke is "light-hearted" (pun intended!), the lesson is obvious, don't over-saturate your text with too many keywords. Make sure your keywords hover at around 2-4% density in the page text, the optimal percentage of keywords to words of narrative. OK, we said we wouldn't try to confuse you by explaining complex concepts like keyword density, and there we went and did it anyway! But this is a significant point. Thousands of marketing experts use oversaturation as a strategy, and it backfires at their client's expense. Just plant keywords on your site in an organic natural way as you talk about your practice and services, and you'll be fine.

Another mission-critical issue is determining whether a competing practice dominates the market using a keyword phrase you are trying to use. If you type your preferred keyword phrase into the bar, and the results come back with your competitor in top slots, it will be challenging (and expensive) to compete with them. What you can do, in that case, is focus on smaller subsets of that phrase. If you choose wisely, you can dominate in the return results of 2 or 3 smaller subsets of a popular keyword phrase and still get more new business than your competitor. Keywords and niche marketing are two of the most important aspects of launching an effective online marketing strategy.

The information in this book is intended to help you become more knowledgeable so that you won't hire an agency, or a consultant, without knowing what questions to ask and how to assess their performance. Use the information provided here to deepen your understanding, so that you can hold people accountable for defining and achieving results.

Everything in this book is critical to understand for a weight loss practitioner looking to take advantage of online marketing. Whether you do the work in-house or hire an outside team, it can be frustrating when marketing doesn't result in new patient calls. It's frustrating for me to hear that also. Most of my clients discover my team after they've spent a fortune and countless hours without getting a single new patient call. Sadly, we hear stories of company owners that have been victims of fraud. Just know that if an online marketing scheme has cheated you, you are not alone.

Not all marketing people are intentionally deceptive. Some genuinely believe that a great website is all you need. Some others just have a limited understanding of how Google works. A lot of DIY in-house marketers work superficially on social media channels, believing that the posts they are putting up provide excellent benefits to the business. But, these efforts aren't enough to bring in new patients. Similar to duplicate content creators or SPAMMERS, many so-called "SEO experts" are just looking to sell something quick and easy. They don't want to take the time to develop a thoughtful long-term strategy for your business.

There are malicious actors out there. We have discovered marketers who have coded a company's website to peddle porn and luxury watches. We've uncovered underhanded tactics are being used to drive useless traffic or put up fake reviews. Don't negotiate with a marketing consultant unless you know what your goals are, and what it will take to reach them.

Ask for client referrals and make them show you precisely how they plan on bringing you new patient calls.

So, now your keywords are selected, the new website is about to be launched. What's next? Blogging for search engine rankings-and dollars!

Just The Facts:

- Keywords are critical; don't bother with trying to rank for your practice name. Rank with keywords that get traffic and are terms that ordinary patients are searching for!

- Incorporate your keywords into your website. Have a webmaster forward a professional-looking URL to the keyword-rich one!

- Specialize, specialize, specialize: don't go for the broad market. Find your niche or specialty and aim towards that!

- Be natural! Google and Bing don't like keyword stuffing; don't ever go over 4% keyword density. Just write naturally.

Chapter 5: Let's Get Local

Blogging and Advanced Local Search Techniques

If you've been following the recommendations in this guide, your online presence is growing, and your site is climbing in the rankings. If other competitors in your market are neglecting their marketing, you may even be at the top. You might also be hearing from new patients. Now the goal is to turn up the volume on these efforts and build up a steady and increasing stream of calls from new patients.

By now, you should have a properly coded website, your Google My Business profile and pages are built out, and your keywords activated. You are poised and ready to rocket to the top of local search results. As much as we appreciate a "go-get-em" approach, I need to issue some words of caution. There is still A LOT of work to do. What we've outlined up to this point is only the beginning. Long-term results that lead to a bustling weight loss practice, or a network of them, requires more. In the vast scheme of things, your website is of little importance to Google compared to bigger players. But, I'm going to share how a local weight loss practice can go toe-to-toe with large organizations and build a significant online presence and higher ranking.

These are advanced local search techniques that allow you to compete with the big spenders and show up right where they are while spending less.

Blogging for Business Growth

The idea that blogging is an integral part of getting to the top of search results might sound crazy, but it's a proven fact. Google has made it very clear that they will give more weight to entities that create and distribute relevant, new content that searchers find useful. This makes sense, given that Internet content has such a short shelf life. In this fast-paced digital world where news and information last for a few minutes, anything you put out there disappears quickly. Yet, newer content is seen as being more valuable, especially where Google is concerned. That's just the world we live in.

Many try to solve this problem by adding new text to their main web pages or swapping out images. They rewrite their About Us page or tweak the services page. This is entirely the wrong approach. Making changes on main pages can lead to coding issues, formatting problems, or having to pay a web developer. And, because you need to update content often, that can get expensive. When practices let their web sites sit and become static, Google stops paying attention. As a result, their online presence sinks like a stone.

Changing content on primary web pages is okay, but it does not boost your ranking that much. And, isn't that the goal? After all, the higher you land in search results, the more likely you'll get seen. Believe it or not, blogging is the answer.

Blogging has a reputation for being a trendy, "activity-du-jour." It seems like everyone, and their cat has a blog. The belief is that blogging will lead to global attention, more status, and money, money, money. It just doesn't work that way. However, set it up correctly, promote it widely, and blogging can be an essential contributor to business success. Yes, blogging is critical to marketing, profitability, and growth. But, it takes considerable effort and expertise to get real results.

The most logical place to house a blog is on your web site. Create a tab for it and update it often. Your blogs must be informative, entertaining, engaging, and original to you. If you follow these rules, Google will love your blog.

Create a space on the site where your posts can be archived and do it during the development phase, not as an add-on. Have a designer create a blog template that's coded and formatted, so every post looks consistent and is easy to publish. A professional template allows you to add new posts without having to deal with HTML, image size, or formatting. It's possible to blow up a site by publishing something that isn't formatted correctly! Publish a new blog every week, or at least bi-monthly. Presto! Fresh, unique content.

Tone & Tasks

As mentioned previously, your clinic must be seen as a trustworthy, professional practice, so that's the general tone your blogs should take. The primary task of search engine crawlers is to find new, relevant content. There's no "silver bullet" that gets practices listed at the top of Google search results. There are no short-cuts. But, blogging, when done well and consistently, can boost your ranking. Put out a fresh and steady stream of useful content, and Google will start to see you as a serious contender in your industry and market.

How often is enough? On average, Google crawlers scan for updates every four hours, 24/7. Does this mean you have to write and publish a blog every four hours? Of course not! However, if several weeks go by, and Google doesn't register anything new, your score starts to drop. To be effective, you have to put something up in a blog post at least once a week. Then, Google will continue to register you as relevant. That can seem daunting and understandably so. If the thought of composing a well-written blog every week isn't appealing, figure something out. It's essential to marketing success and business growth.

Writing an interesting blog post is manageable, writing four a month, not so much.

However, make a schedule and stick with it, and you might find it's a nice break from your work routine. Collect ideas from other posts and keep a running list. Then, when it's time to sit down and write, just look in the Ideas folder. A blog post must be a minimum of 250 words and no more than 800. Longer is better, but they shouldn't be shorter than 250 words. Google won't register it.

If you have time to create and publish two blogs a week, that's fantastic. It's the optimal frequency to earn the most credit from Google. As the search engines scan the Internet and compile data into results, those reports will determine what listings people will see. If Google registers a new piece from you twice a week, you'll begin to show up ahead of other practices in your area.

Pro-tip: Resist the urge to hire a "blog factory" to do the writing! Some paid services will churn out recycled posts for you, but buyer beware. What you gain in quantity will cost you in terms of quality, because the writing won't be original. These services will try to convince you that more is better. It isn't. This approach to blogging can set you back, and you might be in danger of seeing a diminishing rate of return on your investment.

A blog factory, sometimes known as "words for hire," can get you into trouble. Their content isn't specific or unique to your practice, and the blogs are rarely thoughtful or exciting. At times, the material isn't written by someone who speaks the same language as your audience. The factory approach can lead you to lose that new audience you've been working so hard to get. Google doesn't like stolen or recycled content either so, writing one or two original, thoughtful blog posts a week is an excellent investment.

What is Quality Content

We've just established that the quality of the writing matters. A blog that isn't informative, useful, or engaging won't get you the right kind of attention. A good blog post accomplishes two things. First, it tells Google you are a valuable practice in your industry and market. Secondly, when a short introduction to the blog is published on other platforms with a link, it draws people to your site to read the whole thing. A great strategy, this is how you get potential new patients to explore your website and learn more about your practice. The increased traffic tells Google and search engines that you are important and worth listing in search results, a big bonus. Your rankings will just get better and better.

Another question we hear a lot is; How do I make a blog post interesting?

Here are the three things to include:

1) Talk About What You Do
Here is a concept we introduced earlier in the book, writing about what you do, rather than who you are. Don't talk about yourself and your many accomplishments again and again. Potential new patients will tune out. Speak to their interests, their needs, and their concerns. Thoughtful blogs reflect that you know who your likely new patients are. Write blogs that are enlightening, entertaining, or inspiring. Put yourself in their shoes. Talk about what's important to them.

If a new study comes out and debunks a new fad diet, write a medical opinion on why the research is significant. Share a case study of a patient who tried the diet and why it didn't work for them. Or, share why you think the diet could work. Someone who is overweight has very likely tried all kinds of programs and eating plans. Is there a new trend in the industry? Maybe there are rumors about a new superfood that magically speeds up metabolism. Write a blog post titled "Everything You Need to Know About [Superfood] and Weight Loss." Include information from research studies and give your opinion. They will be anxious to learn more, and learn it from you, a trusted medical expert.

That said, you don't want to only focus on weight loss in your blog posts. If you do that, people will eventually tune you out. You need to mix up the blog posts with pieces that are fun or interesting outside of weight loss.

2) Think Global, Act Local

Writing a blog post about your industry is logical, and most practices gravitate to that option. However, there is another lesser-known trick that isn't understood by very many marketers. This tidbit of advice is a super-secret weapon that affects rankings. Write blog posts about local events in your community or share local news and trends. Towards the end of any piece, you can add a paragraph about the work that you do. This local focus is a powerful way to get Google to take notice of your practice and compete with nationally known brands in the rankings.

Here's a great example: Let's say you practice in a city with a well-known food festival. Write a blog about the event and promote it. You can talk about what food will be available. Is there a local chef giving a healthy cooking demonstration, or an organic market giving away free veggie dish samples? Let people know! Write and publish a quick survival guide with tips about finding delicious, low-calorie options at the festival. When you share news about important events in your area, it shows that you are a caring member of their community. This is marketing gold worth mining.

This helps Google because the engines register your practice as one that serves a local area, which they like. This practice of creating and publishing a local blog gives Google lots of keyword clues about your location and business, which improves the quality of returns they are giving to their users, which they love. And, it helps push you up in search results.

Rather than face the tedium of writing blog post after blog post about your services, it's more fun, and beneficial, to move in the opposite direction. Publish general interest pieces not related to weight loss. Someone new to your site will spend more time there because the content has more variety and human interest. This strategy allows you to widen your audience and your competitors are probably not doing this. Using the food festival example, think about how many "foodies," plan to attend the festival and consider how many might have issues with weight loss.

The Center for Disease Control (CDC) in 2019 estimated that one-third of the U.S. population is overweight. If the festival expects 900 people, three hundred of those festival-goers are overweight. Writing an interesting blog post is a fantastic way to reach this new audience, and talk about something that has local interest. You can draw them to your website, encourage them to become patients, and grow your practice.

When new clients sign up with us, many don't have a clear understanding of "thinking globally, but acting locally," so they aren't getting results. The Internet is a vast, complex network where you have to think about being present on a global stage. At the same time, your content must project a local flair. Craft and implement a solid marketing strategy with this in mind, and you will get new patients from the Internet.

Pro Tip: Refer to yourself in blog posts by using your keyword phrase. You don't want to overdo it, but, early on in the article, write something like, "When it comes to weight loss Miami FL, I know visiting the Cuban Food Festival can be a challenge when you are on a diet…" Then, offer some practical advice on how to enjoy the festival while still eating sensibly. The use of keywords in the post will increase its impact on Google and draw a new audience. Some of those who find and read it will become new patients.

Be proactive! Visit local news websites and see what they're covering. Think about trending community topics and how you can link your blog to these various web sites. Search local news outlets to get ideas for posts that have local color and interest. This strategy makes you more likable and down-to-earth, a huge bonus when it comes to building trust with potential new patients. When someone finds your blog and reads through it, it will be an enjoyable experience. They will get practical advice, but also feel a connection to you. Create a sense of familiarity before they meet you, and it will be that much easier for them to call your office to schedule an appointment.

This local approach is a powerful way to make a favorable impression. Potential new patients won't be intimidated, which is often the case. Use the right tone with your content. Let them know they won't be judged; they'll be supported. They won't be lectured; they'll be heard. Diffuse their anxiety and let them know you are a weight loss expert who is kind and approachable. You want potential new patients meeting you online to get a sense that you are part of the community and trustworthy, two great reasons to choose you over a competing weight loss practice. New patients are far more likely to pick up the phone and give your office a call, before any other practice or clinic. That's the real power of blogging.

3) Be Natural

Be natural and authentic. Your main selling point shouldn't be that you are a national figure with a million degrees and professional affiliations. That can be off-putting. I'm not suggesting your content should be sloppy or silly. Of course, you have to be professional. But, inviting new contacts to call for their first appointment requires a conversational approach. Share an anecdote or an authentic customer success story. Google prefers this kind of content, especially when people respond to it.

This personalized method isn't just a Google-specific tactic for new audiences, either. Your existing patients will love you for it too. When they see you online, it confirms that they have made the right choice in becoming your patient. They will feel like they are a part of your "community." This has been a solid marketing principle forever, making a product or service seem accessible, and giving clients a sense of ownership and loyalty to the brand.

If your blog is written well, people will visit your website. If your site is thoughtful, they will imagine themselves losing weight with your help. Consider this a business goal accomplished, thanks to online marketing.

Pro Tip: Make a schedule and a list of topics. That will make it easier when it's time to write your next blog. A good rule of thumb is a 50-50 split. Two blogs about weight loss and two others that are fun, personal, or local.

Marketing studies show that people prefer to do business with a practitioner they know. Studies also show that despite doing research online, people are seeking personal connections. Potential new patients want their problems solved, but they want them solved through personal interaction. Being more personal in your marketing tactics might make you feel a little uncomfortable at first, but it's a strategy that delivers results. If you can use your blog posts to project that you are a practitioner they know and trust, you'll see an increase in new patient calls, and your conversion rates will soar. And blogging will boost your Google ranking. What's not to like?

Just The Facts:

– Blogging is key to the success of your marketing. Make sure to blog at least once a week with a post that is between 250 and 800 words long. If possible, blog twice a week; this is the optimal number.

– Be natural; this will help you be more accessible to your patients, and make you more viewable and indexable by search engines.

Chapter 6: Let's Get Social

Debunking the Myths of Facebook, LinkedIn, YouTube and More

People are very wary of marketing ploys, afraid of being scammed. You may consider social media platforms like Twitter, Facebook, or YouTube useless distractions or a ridiculous waste of time. These social media channels can't possibly help you get new patients and grow a profitable practice.

Or can they?

Hear me out. Your friends, family, patients, basically everyone you know, uses at least one of these platforms, every day! Even those that have a love/hate relationship with social media apps still use them. The fact is, Twitter, Facebook, and social media outlets are here to stay. And, studies indicate they are more relevant than ever, as daily use increases. Love them or hate them; these social platforms are efficient, cost-effective methods for reaching new people and attracting them to your weight loss practice. So you'd better start Tweeting.

Why Social Media?

Social media is a powerful, global force. It impacts culture, social groups, and individuals, it helps Google determine what people are talking about, paying attention to, and what they care about. The one thing every business or product must be is relevant. And, that's the Google scorecard. If your practice doesn't show up in online searches, it's because Google and search engines don't consider your practice important. The Internet is jammed full of bots, scammers, spammers, and article spinners. Marketing sharks look for ways to game the system, pushing out plagiarized content crammed with links, pop up ads, and lots of irrelevant content. In truth, these unethical marketing approaches are useless. Social media users are savvy and perfectly capable of vetting content. Most people aren't about to share or promote posts full of spam on their accounts. They will share content they believe their network of followers and friends will find useful, entertaining, informative, humorous, or engaging. In short, what people look at and share most often on social media is REAL content. The Google algorithm indexes and calculates the relevancy of content based on how often it gets shared by "real people," not bots. You've probably seen headlines about automated distribution systems with fake accounts. This means that Facebook, Google, Twitter, and other social media platforms are under a lot of pressure to be more careful about policing their platforms.

Let me be clear. In some cases, fake content is the result of online marketers out to make as much money as possible, as quickly as possible, without having to work too hard. They have little concern for a client's business growth. They don't care about the profitability of your practice. If a marketer makes promises about search engine results quickly, be wary. They might be using spam or other dark web techniques to get you ranked. This puts your business at risk. When people see irrelevant, viral content invading their feed, they often report it. You can get suspended by Google or kicked off social media platforms. These platforms are laser-focused on getting the user experience right. They aren't going to play around.

When you produce real, original content, the power of these social media audiences is hugely beneficial. Social media success is when real people post real content. Social media users are hungry for posts, articles, tweets, and videos that are valuable enough to warrant a share, like or forward. People love to say, "Hey, check this out," and see reactions from their networks. If you strategically approach this, your content can be the kind of content that gets passed around and seen by thousands of new people.

I call this "exponential marketing power." When someone shares your content with their audience, hundreds of additional people see what you have published. People in that circle share it with their audience, and so on. You can double, even triple your reach in no time at all.

We meet with clients every week who have been trying to avoid social media at all costs. There are many reasons for this. They may lack interest in social media in general, or they're unsure of what people will "comment" on. Many people are anxious about being judged by an audience outside of their inner circle. While it's not uncommon for a business owner to use one or several of these platforms for personal reasons, they fail to see it's usefulness as a marketing tool. This is a big, fat marketing mistake.

When we begin working with clients, the first order of business is to dismantle their deeply-held belief that social media won't lead to business growth. When we dig deeper, we often discover that they hold this belief not because the platforms aren't useful, but because they were taken advantage of by so-called marketing experts. These "experts" didn't know what they were doing or were out to make easy money. They failed to use social media as part of a comprehensive strategy to bring new patients into the practice. These practitioners have, for all practical purposes, become victims of fraud. These are business owners who spent thousands of dollars on schemes that they thought would bring in new business. When it didn't, they lost faith.

There are critical statistics on social media usage and business growth that can't be ignored. One piece of evidence I can offer you is this; The Gen Y demographic (those born between 1965 and 1979) outnumber the Baby Boomers (those born between 1944 to 1964) by quite a margin. In the Gen Y population, 96% are signed on to at least one social network. For most of these people, social media channels are a primary source of information, entertainment, and "social connection."

Ignore social media as a marketing tool, and you miss an opportunity to reach a vast segment of the population. Another statistic; The Gen X demographic spends, on average, 32 hours a week on their devices. Here are additional data making a case for online marketing:

- As of this writing, Facebook has over 2.45 billion active users globally. To put that into perspective, that means Facebook has more users than the entire U.S. population; this is very important in terms of saturation. Active Facebook has 221 million users in the U.S. Twitter has 330 million users worldwide, with 68 million users in the U.S.

- The average time on Google is three minutes. The average time on Facebook is thirteen minutes.

There is plenty more data regarding the increasing popularity of social media platforms, but I'm just trying to make a point. Social media is a powerful force in today's culture and mindset, and therefore, an incredibly powerful marketing tool. And, it's only getting stronger. Google has taken notice of the accelerated growth in social media usage and is responding accordingly. My advice is that you should, too, if you want to grow a weight loss practice.

Social media is here to stay. Every day more people sign up to use these platforms. They want to see and share content, and that includes getting advice and stories from friends and family about an excellent program they have discovered. Their "shares" and posts can consist of messages about your practice if you play your cards right and get creative with your content.

In the next chapter, we're going to take a deep dive into the most critical social networks and share best practices on integrating and linking them to develop an effective online strategy. I'll help you figure out how to approach social media websites and platforms, and use them in a way that Google will take notice. But for now, let's figure out who the biggest players are.

Going Social

There are currently three leading players: Facebook, Twitter, and LinkedIn. This is not to say you should ignore the other platforms. Even smaller, location-based social media platforms like Foursquare, can be useful. However, networks like YouTube, Google My Business, etc. should be the focus of your initial efforts. So, for now, let's explore these three major platforms: Facebook, Twitter, and LinkedIn.

Perfecting your efforts here will allow you to get the most coverage and experience the best Return on Investment (ROI) of time and money. So, let's dig in.

Facebook

Facebook is the biggest platform on the planet, quite literally. This network is the 800-pound gorilla in the room. Everybody knows about it, and most people use it. You will need to capitalize on this fact. Many of you are put off by Facebook's privacy issues. Rumors abound, and the news coverage has not been entirely positive of late. Still, this platform is too large and too widespread to ignore. But how do you start?

The first thing you need is a fan page. Let's look at how to create one and incorporate it into your overall Internet marketing strategy.

Pro Tip: A Business Page for your practice is not the same as a personal page. They operate as separate entities and should not be connected. Nothing you post on your page needs to appear on your business page or vice versa. For those of you resisting Facebook for fear of personal exposure, fear not. Personal information goes on your page and business info on a business page. Set them up correctly, and lack of privacy won't be an issue.

Business pages were set up by Facebook to help organizations and businesses have a presence on the platform using different parameters than those put in place for personal accounts. Facebook Business Pages are very dynamic. They can offer practical information about your practice, share industry news, and provide links to your blog posts. Facebook posts like this are part of the "real and original content" creation we talk about throughout this book.

Find someone well-versed in online marketing to set up your Facebook Business Page. The task is not overly complicated, but if not done correctly, it won't be as effective as it could be. Your webmaster or developer, if they understand online marketing, should be able to help. (And, yes, this is one of the services included in our package).

On your FB page, you'll want viewers to see useful, inspiring stories, articles, and links to the blog posts you've been publishing. The goal is for them to see your page and think, "Hey, I need to lose weight. Maybe this doctor can help." When they see a success story or a review from an existing patient, they'll be intrigued. "How did they do it? How is this different from other weight loss programs?" Bingo! This is how you inspire someone to click on the link to your website.

The goal is to create content on the Business Page that leads people to respond. Millions of people are active in the social media world who surf the Internet daily. While you will only reach a fraction of these users, you can make it a fraction that counts, by posting the right content and setting up the page correctly. This way, you will connect with what we call a "warm" (qualified) lead. Someone who finds you on social media, who is interested in losing weight, and is inspired enough to click through to your website or contact you directly.

Too many marketing amateurs drive traffic to your site that is generated by SPAM. This kind of traffic has zero value in terms of business growth. What you need are pre-qualified, inspired people who come to your website hopeful that your practice will help them.

With research, you can locate geographic areas where a lot of people search for weight loss services. A business page on Facebook can help identify these potential new patients and catch their attention. Because it's location-based, it's beneficial for a local practice like yours. More and more people have smartphones and are using them to view and interact with content. When you put out a Facebook Business page, when people check-in online, they might see your listing. You can include a special offer or discount that will inspire them to act. If you are not using Facebook as a marketing tool, it's time to start! Be creative, interactive, and community-minded. Build a Facebook Business page and find a whole new audience.

Think Links!

Here is perhaps the most important thing to know about social media. Your content on various platforms can be linked to push your ranking higher. You can leverage the unique power of each channel and increase your relevancy score by connecting these platforms in a way that Google recognizes.

Creating and managing a Facebook Business Page, and all of your pages and listings on other platforms requires great attention to detail. It's a lot of work to open accounts, create the profiles, pages or listings, and track all of the passwords so you can go back in to edit them. All of the information, like your business name, address, etc. should be consistent across all platforms right down to the periods and abbreviations. Otherwise, you won't influence your Google ranking. It's critical to seek professional help, someone who understands Google's algorithms and knows how to set up social media accounts and create links.

If you decide on a DIY approach, do lots of research. Learn how to establish your practice on the account, test out what kind of content people respond to most often, and learn how to set up and run analytics. Posts can be scheduled to run 24/7 and be seen by people at all hours, and crawlers can register your content at any time. This requires more than a quick superficial set-up. Profiles, accounts, and content must be strategic to attract a new, qualified audience of potential new patients.

Well, that's about it for Facebook. Once you've got your business page set up, it's time to move on to...

Tweet, Tweet

Twitter is one of the newest and most extensive social networks, and one many shy away from using. Why are so many businesses reluctant to join and use this network? Twitter is an essential tool in your online marketing toolkit because it's the most open social media platform. What do I mean by that? Major players like Facebook and LinkedIn insist that users submit a username and password to log in and view content. There's no such requirement with Twitter. And, unlike other platforms, every single tweet is seen by Google. (A "tweet," for those of you that don't know, is the 280 character message that each user is allowed to submit each time they post.) Google sees all of the tweets in the Twitterverse, so it can track and publish a list of which #hashtags (topics) are trending. Twitter has an enormous influence on search results and rankings. To say it another way, Google uses tweets to help gauge the importance of pages worldwide.

Here is a specific example: pages embedded with links from Twitter are considered more important than pages with links to other platforms. You don't want to SPAM anyone, so don't go crazy, but you should take advantage of this by creating and posting blog posts and content that includes links to tweets. The hidden beauty of Twitter lies in its ability to generate a steady stream of content (brief tweets) without being perceived as SPAM. Facebook allows you to post all day long, but constantly repeating content on that platform starts to feel redundant. Users can get annoyed, may report it, or block you, and you'll lose your audience. On Twitter, however, users expect to see tweets again and again. It's a fast-moving platform, so new tidbits of content pop in and gets replaced within a few seconds, so it seems less intrusive to be repetitive. Twitter allows you to make an impression without triggering a "this is SPAM" mindset.

Once again, you will want to create a regular series of tweets about local events and news, in addition to tweets about your area of expertise to make it more engaging.

Developments in your practice (are you welcoming a new partner or opening a new location?) can be a useful focus of tweets. They can also reflect the concepts you have included in your blog posts. Shorten the central idea down to 280 characters and send it out with a link. Tweets can go out once or twice a day, as opposed to blogs that are published once a week.

If you have been avoiding this platform, creating a series of tweets to go out each day can seem daunting. However, a 280 character message isn't much, and tweets can be shorter. It's not that much work. You can create and distribute tweets using scheduling and distribution tools.

Identify a list of relevant topics, find an hour or so in your week, and use it to write enough tweets to last the week. Write fifteen or twenty messages, schedule them, and get back to work! Don't study what other people are tweeting, that's an unnecessary time suck. And, don't spend hours and hours sweating, thinking you have to create the perfect tweets. Just make them interesting enough, and move on.

Pro Tip: Don't tweet only links to your blog post without text. When linking Tweets to your blog posts, include a short phrase or phrases that indicate what the topic is, but don't do a direct copy and paste. Then at the end of the Tweet, include a link to the blog on your web site.

Countless blogging platforms offer plugins. These allow you to send out tweets automatically, with links, to the blog you are creating. Take advantage of this kind of tool to lighten your workload. It isn't SPAM because blog posts only come out once a week. These are convenient tools for consistently getting content out there with links that will lead people to your website. These blogging tools usually offer plugins to other platforms as well. Distribute posts about your blog to Facebook, or learn how to push your stuff out to LinkedIn. Take advantage of these automated sharing tools and get your blog content out on Twitter, Facebook, LinkedIn, Instagram, etc., and watch your online presence grow!

LinkedIn

LinkedIn is a powerful tool that has been entirely overshadowed by its bigger social media cousins, Facebook and Twitter. LinkedIn is mainly a professional networking tool and resume-sharing site. It is grossly underutilized as a marketing tool, which works to your advantage. If you are not using LinkedIn, you are missing out on a great opportunity. This social platform can become a strong foundation for business growth if you learn how to use it.

As an organization, LinkedIn is no slouch. It is publicly traded (LNKD) and has a market cap of $8-$10 billion (or $70-$100 per user). This makes it a formidable and fast-growing contender in the social media sphere. And, this channel has an added attraction. Because of its status as a site for financially sound professionals looking to network, share business news, or make a job change, the average LinkedIn user is likely to have expendable income. Here are a few facts about the LinkedIn audience:

Over one-fifth of users work at a level of middle management or above
Almost 60% have a college or postgraduate degree
Average Household Income is $88,573.

What does this all have to do with weight loss? Let me put it this way: LinkedIn is a vast audience of professionals who are "wealthy" and are highly educated. They aren't on the network looking for cat videos or silly home movies. These are no-nonsense adults interacting with each other by sharing knowledge and ideas that have real value. They are professionals prepped and ready to be introduced to your practice and services if they are presented in the right way.

LinkedIn is about creating and controlling messages about your industry, practice, and services. Be exciting but professional, and give people content worth sharing. This platform delivers a bigger, broader audience, full of people who have the means to pay for your services.

Press Releases

Technically, creating and distributing press releases isn't a social media practice. We include it here because press releases are an excellent way to cross-promote your practice on social media platforms.

Press Releases are overlooked as a marketing tool. They can be shared widely and receive comments from people, just like other forms of content. One little known secret; in the case of press releases, it's the one time Google expects to see exact duplicate content. The more "copied," and shared a press release is in its original form, the more valuable Google will perceive it.

The idea of writing a press release might seem intimidating. Clients often think they don't have news big enough to share in this way. I'm here to tell you that you do. Here are 15 easy ideas for press releases:

You are speaking at an industry conference, local chamber of commerce, rotary club, etc. Let everyone know!

You have hired someone new in your practice. Introduce them.

Someone in your organization has been promoted

Your practice has joined an association (local or national) or received an award

You are offering a new service or product

You have a new office, or you've expanded your practice

Successful Treatment -- write a Case Study about an existing patient and share their success story.

Your practice is being recognized by local or national industry or association

An employee is being honored at a charity benefit or is joining the board of directors at a non-profit

You have signed on to sponsor a charity benefit

Your service ties into a current, trending event (a new law, health discovery, a fitness trend, or a movie release, etc.)

You've launched a new website

The release of a special report in your industry where you are quoted

Paid and free sites exist where you can submit a press release and get it published. A paid site can be worth it, depending on your situation. They will forward your announcement to respected news distribution sites like the Associated Press and newswire services like Yahoo and Google News. The wider the distribution, the better chance you have of getting it published elsewhere.

Interestingly enough, using a more extensive, national distribution network is the best way to get covered by a local outlet. National news distribution sites are where local news organizations go to troll for story ideas. You can take advantage of national distribution to get local coverage.

As mentioned previously, filters are there to weed out redundant (SPAM) content. However, when content is categorized as a press release, these filters don't apply. Duplicating and repeating content as it is written is the norm. Big names like the Associated Press and Reuters will source duplicate content in a press release, so you bypass the filters, no problem.

Google

What makes Google different from Facebook, Linkedin, Youtube, and Twitter? First, we need to summarize how these four major players came to be and the technical details of how they operate. We have to explore that first if you are to understand Google My Business.

YouTube

Let's start with YouTube. If I make a video and publish it, people can search for it, watch it, share it, and comment on it. As a search-based network, this is a very open platform, the most accessible of them all. Subscribing to a channel is different from just browsing on it. Very few people use the subscribe function on YouTube as a social element.

LinkedIn

Next up is LinkedIn, which began as a platform where people could promote their resume, or find jobs or candidates for job openings. While LinkedIn's function is promoting one's professional skills, it is also used to collaborate, share information, gather news from thought leaders, and build groups in specific industries.

You can log in to LinkedIn and get a question answered, find articles written by your favorite business executives, or share recent professional successes to others. LinkedIn is the most closed network of the four big players. You have to know someone's email to send them an invitation to connect. It helps if you have worked with them before, or you both belong to a professional group. Anyone that subscribes to the platform can follow someone, even a high profile executive, like Bill Gates. However, you must seek and gain permission using the LinkedIn messaging tool before you can include them in your network.

Twitter

With Twitter, I can push information out to as many people as I like, and it spreads quickly. Google indexes each tweet, which is a bonus. Anyone on Twitter can hit "follow" on my profile, and they'll be added to my account and see my updates. I don't have to allow them to follow me, but

I can block them if I don't want them in my network. And I don't have to follow them back. This means communication on Twitter, at times, can be a one-way conversation.

Tweets are brief tidbits of information (the Tweet limit is 280 characters) sent out in short bursts. Some users create "threads" by sequencing several tweets in a row. Interactions on twitter involve replying to others' tweets, commenting, or retweeting messages onto your account. You can also imbed links to a video, blog post, press release, or other content as you see fit. The goal is to gather like-minded followers and gain influence.

Facebook

Facebook is the king of social media platforms. It was the first platform to attract a massive list of subscribers. Facebook is about "friending" someone. You and I must agree to "like" each other to share information. As they post or share content, many assume that everyone in their network will see it on their newsfeeds, but this is not always the case. When it comes to Facebook, users are not in control of what pops into their feed because the network has developed a sophisticated algorithm, called Edge. Edge controls all of the information on the platform. Based on what you click on and respond to, share, and comment on, Facebook determines what you will see next. The usefulness of Facebook for business is the business page option.

Google

What makes Google different?

Google was not built as a social media platform. The goal was to give people a way to connect all of their devices and store their content, like photos, documents, and spreadsheets, in one place. You can create something in one application, save it over to Google and share it. Or, it can stay private. This is simply cloud computing on a major scale. Google made it possible to store everything in one place and share it, which was convenient. For anyone in marketing, it was a fantastic promotional tool.

Then came Google+, the company's effort to expand into a social platform. They developed a feature called Circles to control the stream of information in and out of Google+. Users could build a personal network and organize the connections into "buckets." For example, you could group work contacts and family contacts into different circles.

The Google+1 button was created so people could share news and information they liked to their circles. It also became a way for marketers to share products and services. Google+ gave people the power to create and distribute content. It included an option to schedule a video chat for up to ten people. You could display content on the "walls" you created as part of your account, and share it. There was an added advantage to this platform because it was built to accommodate large-format images, something other platforms can't accept.

Google intended to make it easier for people to navigate between all of the Google functions and features, tie in their content, and share it all using the Google+ social platform.

The only problem? Google+ didn't take off as a social network. One theory is that the tool did not offer a good user experience. It was too difficult to navigate. Then, in October of 2018, there was a security breach affecting over 100,000 users. This dealt Google+ the final death blow. As of August of 2019, Google+ is no longer operating as a social networking platform.

Press Releases

As we mentioned previously, press releases are an essential part of any successful online marketing strategy. We take the task of writing, publishing, and syndicating press releases very seriously. For our clients, it has become an effective way for us to help them rise in the search results and bring in new patients. We find that our average client has more important things to focus on than writing press releases, so we also offer this valuable service. And, we have a massive distribution network, to ensure wide release. If and when you begin to understand how much of a competitive advantage press release campaigns can offer, you'll commit to making them an integral part of your marketing.

Get Access To Our Professional Social Media Team That Will Create 30 Days Of Social Media Content ($499 Value) For FREE: http://weight-loss-social.com

The Only Constant is Change

The real challenge of social media is that the platforms and technology are constantly changing. The dismantling of Google+ is a perfect example. Our goal is to make sure that our subscribers can access the most relevant, up-to-date information about all of these platforms and tools. Search engine algorithms, privacy rules, security breaches, acceptable content rules, new distribution tools, the changes that can impact your marketing are endless.

Our clients are always in the know if they care to be. By using our "Free Resources" option, you can research all of the latest changes and news impacting your marketing efforts. Simply sign up with us, and make use of the links we provide. Stay up-to-date on social platforms, filters, search engine algorithms, privacy rules, and more. You will always be in the know about the latest and greatest news that impacts online marketing.

With that, our foray into social media has ended. Next, we'll help you navigate the complexity of directory listings.

Just The Facts:

- Social media is one of the most important forces in marketing today: it can't afford to be ignored, and you need to set up strategies for dealing with it.

- The three biggest social media players right now are Facebook, Twitter, and LinkedIn: you need to have pages for them and have a system set up on your blog that pushes blog updates to the respective social networks.

- Don't forget Google My Business. Incorporate it into your strategy!

- Press releases are a vital part of your online marketing strategy, so much so that you should have your marketing business do it for you and cut down on the immense amount of time you're spending on it.

- Social media is rapidly changing, and no single strategy will stay effective forever; make sure to keep yourself updated to stay ahead of the game!

Chapter 7: Out With The Old

How to Use Online Directories to Get More Patients

If you became an Internet user before online searching became a thing, you'd recognize the term "directory listings." That's because directory listings are online versions of old fashioned print directories, like the Yellow Pages or White Pages.

Services like SuperPages, YellowPages.com, Yahoo Local, Bing Places, and Google My Business are all business listing directories (listings are sometimes called "citations," by marketers). These directories help ordinary people find products and services based on a topic or industry. The challenge of listing with these sites is choosing between the thousands available. It takes a considerable amount of time to select and register with them. How many do you list with? Should you pay for a listing or focus on free directories? These are just a few of the questions people have about directory listings.

Here are some answers.

There are twelve to fifteen major players where you must list your weight loss practice. These directory sites carry more weight with search engines, and they feed their data to the smaller directories. For this reason, listing with the top players is a must. In addition to the main directories like MerchantCircle.com, SuperPages.com, Yelp.com, and Yahoo Local, weight loss practices should also get listed on sites relevant to health or weight loss sites, such as HealthGrades.com.

The majority of these services allow you to subscribe and list your practice for free. However, eventually, they will attempt to upsell you by offering additional reach through a paid service. YOU DO NOT NEED THESE ADD-ONS, especially in the beginning. As soon as you list with a directory, the sales calls will start. Resist the urge.

The paid options they offer might be helpful down the road, but you won't know which ones are worth the investment until you launch your overall strategy. Once you create accounts on the primary sites and establish metrics that measure the results, you can consider adding paid features.

Pro Tip: Do not pay for add-on services offered by Local Directory companies until your online presence and strategy are in place.

Please, if you don't follow any other piece of advice we give you, heed this warning! You must first establish a baseline of success in terms of ranking and new business growth. Once you are capable of running meaningful analytics regarding traffic from these sites, you can consider paid options. You must first establish a baseline of success in terms of ranking and new business growth, and the contribution the listing site has made to that growth. You have to know what it costs to get each new patient and what each patient is worth over time. Once you can identify which platforms and distribution networks bring you the most qualified traffic, you can try some of their paid services. Still, without analytics, you won't know which directories are benefitting the bottom line.

Some directories, like InfoUSA, are more influential. You must be listed there, and your profile has to be correct and optimized. Most smaller directories will pull your data from InfoUSA, so if your information isn't optimized there, it will trickle down and be incorrect everywhere. You certainly don't want that! Please make sure that your business information on InfoUSA and the other major directories is correct in every detail.

Later, additional services or additional paid directory listings can be considered on a case-by-case basis. Directories/citations have risen in importance because of recent updates Google made to local search return policies (the local search rules outlined in chapter 1). The new algorithm is designed to register where you are located, using your listings as a guide. It will use this information to decide whether you are important enough to deserve a spot on Google My Business. If you haven't filled out and claimed your profile, you'll miss out on this excellent opportunity for increased visibility!

Ever since Google began showing local search returns alongside global searches, it's possible to rank on the front page with larger businesses. However, this means pushing out "weighted" content, which includes additional local directory listings.

By making sure your practice lists in five, ten, or fifteen directories, with reviews from locals, it's quite likely that your practice can place very well in

Google's ranking system. We'll discuss the importance of patient reviews in the next chapter, but for now, suffice it to say, directory listings with reviews are even more powerful.

Pro tip: We encourage clients to list their weight loss practice on as many directories as possible. You can hire a service to do this for you, but it's best to do it manually. This way, you have full control over every detail. Remember, larger directories feed smaller ones, so if a mistake gets made, it spreads like wildfire. Fixing this problem is very time-consuming. You don't want a robotic data entry service populating this critical information about your business.

Just find a list of the top directories and enter all of the data that is requested. Include every photo where there is an option to do so. Add the required titles, fill out every box, and double-check every detail. Be consistent when it comes to abbreviations, the company name, any numbers, etc. You must use your keywords in the title and geolocation in the description (geolocation is just an SEO term for city/state.) In keeping with the weight loss example, if your primary keyword phrase is "WeightLossMiami.com." that must be included.

DIY and Directory Listings

It's relatively easy to list your practice. You visit the directory's website, create an account (make sure you track your user name and passwords!), and submit all of the information about your practice, entirely and carefully. As we have mentioned previously, focus on the free sites first.

Warning: Directory companies will try to upsell you on additional paid services. Check with a knowledgeable, independent marketing professional before signing up for any paid service enhancements. These will involve monthly or yearly fees that can add up. It will end up being very expensive if it fails to bring in new patients. When submissions are made correctly on free directories, there isn't a need to enlist in "pay-to-play" services. Judicious and skillful use of keywords and geolocation on free directory services will be more than enough to bump you up in the rankings.

We have many clients ranked at the top of "Google My Business" who have never paid to be listed. At times, we do recommend a paid service enhancement, but that's if metrics are showing it's bringing in traffic. Please don't pay for "extra" services from local directories, in the beginning, and especially without professional guidance.

Be warned: Unfair sales tactics are being practiced by companies you might think are reputable. Sham marketers pretend to be associated with the Better Business Bureau or claim to reach millions of people, without telling you whether it's qualified traffic. The changes Google has made, along with more strict policies being implemented across the board, means directories have had to rethink their business model. They are scrambling for revenue and will use underhanded measures to get you to sign up. They will call you every day, play upon your fears, send threatening letters, or make false promises about boosting your ranking. Sadly, it has come to this, and you must be on your guard.

The one thing these directories won't do is offer you proof that your listing is triggering calls to your practice. That's because they can't. They don't have the metrics. In any case, it's not necessary to pay for directory listings or add-on services. It's entirely possible to get ranked using free services.

So, keep pursuing free listings. Stay the course and implement the online marketing strategies outlined in this book, and you won't need to pay for directories or their add-ons.

Pro Tip: You must list your entity as a single business, at one address. A problem we see time and time again, especially with medical professionals, is when doctors share a space. If four or five practitioners all try listing their practices using the same address, it won't work. When Google queries the directory listings, it gets confused. Google will assume you're trying to game the system by putting out duplicate listings. Instead of ranking, every practice or doctor associated with the address will be ignored. Points will be lost with Google, points you can't afford to lose if you want to show up on top. Be meticulous and submit only one listing at one address. Be smart and search your business to see the information that is out there. Search the names of doctors in your office suite and see if they've registered with your address. If they have, you will have to delete all of the listings and start over, which is a considerable amount of work. If, for any reason, you can't delete multiple listings, get it down to one and edit it as best you can.

Creating duplicate listings is a trick that some marketers use to boost rankings. Google cracks down heavily on this method because it doesn't serve its users. Remember: duplicate listings are counterproductive! Too many and Google will ignore your listing or worse, suspend your accounts. Do your research when hiring SEO firms and be careful.

Another word of advice regarding directory listings is to use your full set of keywords and geolocation in the "description" sections. Directories often provide space to include both short and long descriptions of your services. This is excellent because you can share what your practice is all about. It makes sense to include your keywords in those description boxes. However, you don't want to jam your business name with multiple keywords in the "Company Name" box, or a "Company Title" box. Google views this as "keyword stuffing" and will ignore your listing.

Follow the directions in this guide carefully. Use your business name (that should already exist), the one with a keyword and geolocation (i.e., DrSmithWeightLossPhoenixAZ." This way, you are submitting a keyword-rich URL. If you've created a URL without a keyword, go ahead and submit it, but be aware you won't experience the same ranking benefits. Don't jam your business name with multiple keywords or several geolocations. Google will ignore your practice when building search results, which will hurt you in the long term.

Savvy marketing experts select business names with ONE keyword phrase and ONE location. Google does not like blatant keyword stuffing in business titles. A name like "Jones-Smith Barney Chiropractors Back Pain Neck Pain Dallas Texas" will get you penalized. It's a poor choice of a business name, and it doesn't make a proper URL. Multiple keywords belong in the practice description, not the business name.

Directory listing services may suggest keywords as you fill out your listing. Consider using them. They are probably very similar to categories you are used to seeing everywhere. Some directories give you space to type in your keywords, in which case you should do so. But don't go crazy! Google values up to 3-4 keywords per description, but anything after that will look like you are gaming the system, and they'll ignore it.

Here is a list of the most important directories where your practice MUST be listed:

Google My Business
Yahoo!

YellowBot
Yelp
WhitePages
MapQuest
SuperPages
CitySearch
Yellowbook
Local.com
MerchantCircle

There are over forty directories we subscribe to on behalf of clients, depending on their location. Some of these are relevant now but will be less so a year from now. Changes in the market, and the metrics we track over time, can lead to a need to make adjustments. To get started, just research and select fifteen industry-specific directories (in addition to those listed above).

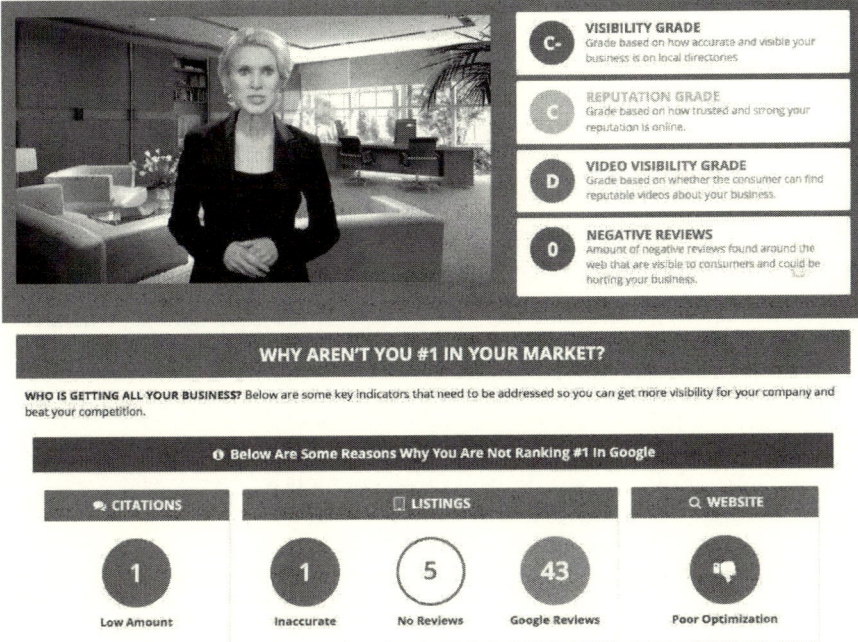

FREE Local Directory Business Report

Look for relevancy in your industry and complete a profile and listing by filling in every box. Upload photos and videos as requested. Do this consistently across all listings, and then mark it on your calendar to revisit these sites every few months. This way, you can see if there has been any misinformation propagating or, if you need to make changes to get more traction.

Google My Business

Google My Business is not technically a directory, but it warrants special mention here.

Pro Tip: The Google listing should be the last thing you create! Get the rest of your directory listings published and wait at least one month. The order is critical, so much so, that if we take on a client who already has a Google listing, but not other directory listings, we delete everything and start over.

Google crawlers are out there searching the entire Internet to register information. Completing this monumental task takes them about four months. Then, it starts again. Google looks for directory listings, blogs, patient reviews, posts, traffic, everything. However, Google registers its accounts first. Your ranking is affected by this, a fact very few people are aware of. As you wait for the four-month cycle and Google to register your Google listing, hold off on other directory listings. You'll want to give Google time to recognize your core account.

A Word About Adwords

Another powerful, yet rarely discussed advertising approach is Pay-Per-Click advertising. The most well-known example of this is Google AdWords. Using the AdWords feature is the quickest way to get your business listed on Page #1 of Google. You can do it in 10 minutes or less, and it will only cost you a few dollars a day IF YOU KNOW WHAT YOU ARE DOING! Otherwise, it can be costly.

If you don't understand how to use Pay-Per-Click advertising, you might waste thousands of dollars for clicks from unqualified traffic, visitors who will never become patients. One important note is to make sure your ads are shown ONLY in your geographical area. Find someone skilled at AdWords placement and pay them to put your ads in the right spaces. Paid ads can be targeted to specific, pre-qualified audiences and will result in a better return. Ad words can bring in new business, but only if a knowledgeable person manages the process.

Chapter 8: In With New Reviews

How Online Reviews Drive Results & Build Your Reputation

One aspect of online marketing that is completely underestimated is the power of collecting and publishing positive reviews. What I'm talking about here are authentic reviews from real people, feedback that is detailed, and describes a positive experience a patient has had at your practice. A lot of practitioners think that patient reviews have minimal impact on business growth. Nothing could be further from the truth.

Weight Loss Clinic

By: Kimberly W.

★ ★ ★ ★ ★

What a great weight loss program. Since I starting the program I have lost 35 pounds. When I first came to see the doctor I really did not know if they were going to be able to help me. I had tried so any different programs, pills and routines. Keto, South Beach nothing was really helping. I was tired every day and I could hardly even walk across the room without getting winded. When I came here everyone was so nice. They listened to me and got me started the first day. The program is super easy and I think that anyone who follows the program will loose weight.

Become Our Next Satisfied Patient
Call Us Today At
212-956-5920

Reviews can make or break search engine rankings. Positive reviews build your reputation and inspire trust in potential new patients who discover you online. Excellent reviews are just the thing to trigger click-throughs to your website or a phone call. Positive reviews also influence Google's ranking system, tipping the scales in your favor.

A bad review should be viewed as constructive feedback, a way for business owners to uncover aspects of their practice that need improvement. Reviews are valuable because they make it easy for someone to believe that your practice is the one to call.

Again, remember that 97% of people seeking weight loss services will do so online first. Also, a good reminder, Google uses reviews to judge the authenticity of a business or practice. Reviews indicate to Google that you are a real practitioner serving in your local market. They will assess positive review data to determine your ranking, but too many negative reviews can hurt your placement.

Google is pretty darn good at assessing whether a review is from a real person. Real (not fake) reviews tend to have detailed information and particular use of language. There are details about their visit that someone would not be able to make up. It might involve interactions with staff, the quality of care, wait times, or the office environment. These reviews affect the impression people will have about your practice as they look at your online listing. And, reviews help Google determine where to rank your business.

There are many review sites out there, with Yelp being one of the most well-known. Some of these sites allow people to award stars, which have even more influence. Google scrapes these numbers and does a website "litmus test." They decide where your practice should rank, in part, based on the average number of stars you have in your reviews. Reviews have become so valuable to Google that they adjusted their user interface to display a "Write a review" button prominently in their system. The button encourages people who have interacted with your practice to write an honest review on the Google platform.

R&R: Reviews and Your Reputation

There are plenty of sites that offer a review feature; they all function similarly. Google reads the review data from all of these sites and uses it to weigh the importance of your online presence. If you know how you can use reviews to push your business higher in search results. And the higher your ranking, the more people will see your listing. Once they see your listing, good reviews will prompt them to call your practice or visit your website.

The competing practices in your area are probably not actively pursuing positive reviews. Most practices don't. That's because they fail to recognize the marketing potential that positive reviews have. We've done extensive research on this, specifically in medical weight loss. Very few clinics use reviews as part of their marketing strategy, so doing so will give you a significant advantage.

As you can see in the illustration above, two practitioners have one review each, and the rest have zero. With just a few positive patient reviews, your practice would rise to the top of this list. It requires a bit of work, but work that pays off in new patient calls. Collect just a few patient reviews every month, do it consistently for a few months, and make significant progress. You'll see your practice rise in Google search results and start to get more calls.

The first essential task is assessing how many reviews will be needed to rank higher. You can research competing practices by typing your keywords into the Google search bar. Then, for the businesses that pop up, look at the number of reviews they all have. If the first listing with reviews has six reviews, you'll need to get ten. If they have twenty, you'll have to collect forty, and so on.

Typically, weight loss practitioners in densely populated areas have somewhere between 15 and 20 reviews. There are many markets where practices haven't bothered to do this at all. No matter what the results are in your area, to play the rankings game, you will have to double the number of reviews your competitors have in the "local" box. If they don't have any, it won't be hard to rank higher.

Don't let the idea of reviews intimidate you. I'll share with you later why there is no reason to fear putting your practice out there for people to comment. In the meantime, let's talk about the challenge of the process itself. Ours is a measured approach, slowly gathering reviews over time. For example, if the practice needs twenty reviews, consider collecting and publishing four or five each month. That's manageable, right? Especially when you use our pre-packaged system.

Before we talk about collecting positive feedback, we first have to take a look at review sites.

Setting Your Sites

One question we get asked a lot is which review sites to focus on. There are so many sites that offer a review feature. Because you are asking patients for a favor, you want to make it as easy as possible for them. Keep in mind that many local directory sites allow visitors to publish reviews. For this reason, it makes sense to send some patients to directory sites where you already have a listing. Search engines weigh various review sites differently. For example, Yelp is considered one of the most important sites, and reviews there carry more weight. You'll have to come up with a formula for reputable review sites, and combine that with lesser-known places where it might be easy to get your patients to leave their comments.

Thankfully, this is a reasonably efficient and straightforward process. First, do a Google search using your keywords and location. Once you have submitted the search phrase, scan the results until you find returns from review sites.

They will look something like this: https://www.yelp.com > New York, NY > healthy weight loss NYC. Don't dig too far down; just find the top four or five listings that come from review sites. For example, if you were a weight loss physician in Denver, you could type "Healthy Weight Loss Denver, Co." in the search box. The results might include listings from Yelp and Google. The first three to five listings that appear from review sites are the ones to focus on. Those will be the links you include in your request to patients when you ask them for a review. If you don't find any listings in the search results that are from review sites, you can just go right ahead and direct patients to the most well-known reviews sites. As a word of caution, this review strategy has to be implemented along with all of the other recommendations in this guide to have any impact. But it does work. It just requires patience.

To put things in perspective, every day, some 10,000 new websites are published. It takes months for search engine crawlers to index all of this new data, along with updates. If you plug away at some of the highly ranked review sites and manage to get some positive reviews, that's a start. This can take months. However, Google will eventually register these reviews and attribute them to your online presence. Get a few more reviews on a few more sites, and you could start to see your practice rise in the rankings. Just be aware, this doesn't happen overnight.

Pro Tip: If a competing practice is ranking in your keyword niche, and they have lots of reviews, just focus on two review sites to start. Ordinarily, weight loss practitioners don't deal with this issue. Local markets aren't usually saturated with reviews, good or bad. When Google or a search tool is comparing your practice with another, the engine will look at the keywords and determine which review sites show up. For example, if your keyword niche is "back pain," and the majority of reviews are from CitySearch, that's where you can direct your patients to leave reviews.

Once you've narrowed down the directories or review sites to target, you can solicit patients and ask them to create and post reviews on your behalf.

Getting Rave Reviews

Of course, your outreach should start with longer-term clients, because they are obviously happy with your services and will be more likely to write a review. At the same time, it doesn't hurt to ask newer patients as well, as long as they have had a positive experience.

I understand if you are feeling reluctant about soliciting patients for reviews. Asking for testimonials can be uncomfortable, but my instinct tells me that you will be pleasantly surprised to find your patients like doing business with you. Think about how nice it will be to discover that you have patients willing to submit positive feedback on your behalf!

Because this is a challenging process, we developed an efficient system that makes it easy for our clients to ask for patient reviews.

Warning: You should not, under any circumstances, go to a review website and create fake reviews for your practice!

You cannot produce and publish reviews pretending to be a patient. Furthermore, you can't ask them to give you their feedback, and then submit it yourself. You can't hire a consultant to create fake reviews, either.

Google reads every single IP address that generates reviews. If a search engine sees multiple reviews coming from the same IP, they'll ignore them. In a worst-case scenario, breaking the review rules can result in Google deleting your listing altogether. When they see multiple reviews about one business coming from the same IP, it triggers a review of your practice and possibly suspension from Google!

You can't take a real review written by an actual patient and copy it word-for-word into a review site from your IP, either. It will get flagged. You can't sit patients down in your office and ask them to write reviews on your computer before leaving. It still comes in from your IP.

A typical scam marketing consultants run is hiring a team to sit and flood sites with fake reviews. This is SPAM and Google is continuously, diligently working to eliminate it. Any review coming from your IP address is invalid and may cause you to be penalized, which ruins your chances of showing up in search results. Too many submissions coming from a single IP address, even if it's not yours, is a problem. While this may seem unfair, you can't blame Google. Blame the businesses and sham marketers who have gone before you, submitting hundreds of fake reviews they wrote themselves. This is a crucial takeaway from this book, so please heed the advice.

The only way to get authentic reviews is to cheerfully and respectfully ask for them! Patients must be willing to go home, to their computer, and write a review for your practice. Make it as easy as possible. Direct them to specific sites, and give them a few sample reviews as a writing guide. Lead them to places where they already have accounts, so Google identifies the review with a valid email. Create a special offer as a thank you.

If this sounds like work, it is, which is why so many practices fail to do it. However, the results will far outweigh any inconvenience.

Pro Tip: Be careful when hiring an outside firm to manage the review process. Countless marketing firms promise to solicit reviews on your behalf. Too often, these services use devious methods. They spin fake reviews internally and post them from one IP address. This is considered fraud. Be very careful about who you consult with when it comes to using reputation marketing to improve your SEO ranking. If a company claims they can get you twenty reviews in a week, you'd better ask a lot of questions.

We had a practice come to us for help because the so-called "experts" they hired had published twenty reviews on their behalf, and they were all identical! These consultants just altered the first line of text and added a fake patient name. The rest of the feedback was exactly the same. This approach didn't fool anyone, least of all, Google.

Hiring the wrong reputation marketing team had cost the client dearly, and it took us a considerable effort to make it right. I don't want that to be you. If you hire outside help, make sure that they are 100% transparent about the process, and that they are a proven agency or trusted partner. Do they, themselves, have favorable reviews? That's an excellent place to start.

While positive reviews are fine for the ego, they're even better for search engine rankings and earning the trust of people searching online. It's five-star reviews that can trigger calls from new patients.

Because the review process is so crucial to marketing success, we manage the entire process for our clients. We produce the cards (including designing and mailing them), we oversee a system that places phone calls to follow-up, and we work closely with your staff. It's our job to support them as they solicit reviews. Then, we report back on all the positive reviews that come in. We play an active role in this process because of the sensitive nature of patient reviews. In the rare case of a negative review, we'll help strategize how to minimize its impact.

In the end, no matter who you choose to work with, make sure they stay close to your practice and give you plenty of good advice about the review process and building up your reputation online. It's very important.

For us, reputation marketing is the white-glove service our clients have come to expect, and it's the high-quality support you deserve. If you'd like, you can set up an automated review solicitation service by visiting http://weight-loss-reputation.com. By getting this book, you qualify to visit this URL and gain free access to an exclusive in depth review assessment and proven system. Please note, this review process is valid and can bring in new patients, but significant business growth only happens when you implement the entire strategy, all of the steps outlined in this book.

For a limited time, we are offering our review system for free. However, our ability to monitor the process for those who are not full-service clients will be on a first-come, first-served basis. Collecting reviews, publishing them on the right sites, and getting Google to recognize them takes time. There are times when it will take longer for us to send you the materials and progress reports. Still, this free offer is a tremendous opportunity to have my expert team review your online presence and help you develop a review system that will bring in new business.

Count the Ways

One of the easiest ways to get reviews is to hand out review cards to your patients. But, using only one mode of communication to solicit reviews isn't enough. You can also mail a review request to their home, send follow-up emails, or send a reminder text.

The requests should always be friendly and brief. Simply tell your patients that reviews are essential to the growth of your practice. Ask them to submit a review and give them links to follow. Give them a sample review so they can imagine how easy it is. You can generate empathy by showing patients where you rank and explain that you'd like their help to rank higher so you can help more people lose weight. Enlist the help of your current patients to spread the word about your practice. If you are a good practitioner, they'll be happy to do so!

Another critical thing to mention about reviews is the importance of diversification. You'll need to get reviews published on several different directories and review sites. There's Google My Business, Yelp and CitySearch, just to name a few. It's best to have reviews on various sites because then Google will rank your business higher. Change out the links you include on your review request cards. List Yelp on some, CitySearch on others, and so on. Be sure to include review sites specific to your industry. And, don't put more than one or two links on a card. It gets confusing. Keep things clean and straightforward, but switch out the suggested review site link each time you get cards printed.

The same goes for review solicitation emails. Patients may already have accounts set up with a review site like Yelp, so include a variety of links with review site suggestions. A patient is more inclined to log on and submit feedback if you include links, especially if they see a site they've used in the past. If they are an active participant on that site, their comments will hold more weight, because Google will know a real person has submitted it. And, reviews don't need to be long. A brief narrative from a patient detailing their visit, what it's like to work with you, or the results they have achieved is quite enough.

It can be scary to put your practice up for criticism but take heart. More often than not, practitioners find that there are already positive reviews out there, and patients are more than willing to help. Frame your request as a "one for the team" effort. Thank them for being your patient; let them know that you value their business. Then ask them to help spread the word!

This review process plays a significant role in online marketing success. Positive feedback is a driving force behind increasing Google My Business rankings. By putting a system in place that will create a steady stream of positive reviews for your practice, you're ensuring a steady climb to the top of search engine results.

Chapter 9: The Magnetic Practice

The Components of Successful Traffic Campaigns

A word about traffic: when it comes to business, there is nothing more important. Brick and mortar storefronts call it foot traffic. In the digital world, traffic describes the number of people who visit a business online. This includes social media platforms, video channels, anyone who clicks on a blog post or newsletter, or a website visit. If someone sees or interacts with an online portal you own, it's considered traffic.

Websites, Facebook posts, YouTube videos, or Google My Business pages can all generate traffic. People can also find a practice through a directory listing or review site. A business has a great deal of control over its online portals. Sadly, few pay any attention at all to these powerful tools that can be used to attract new business. The right content on the right platforms, if consistently and frequently refreshed, can transform a business, and yet, many owners continue to say they don't care about their online presence.

The goal of marketing on the Internet should be to get as many people as possible to see your content and call for an appointment. This is the only traffic metric that matters. The goal isn't to get as much generic traffic as possible. The goal is to get the right kind of traffic, qualified visitors that result in new business gains.

Generating qualified traffic is part art, part science. The tools needed to do it effectively include email, social media platforms, and search listings that include patient reviews. We must add to that list; paid traffic. Results-driven marketing involves a careful balance of general (but interesting) content, promotion of services, but today, you can't make it without some "pay to play" services. If the investment in paid traffic is managed well, it can change everything. However, it is possible to throw tons of money at paid Adword campaigns or Facebook Boosts and end up with nothing to show for it. It's about how it's set up, and whether analytics are a part of the equation.

Email Marketing

Email is still one of the most powerful ways to get a practice, and its services, in front of the right people. In my experience, every business understands that they need a monthly newsletter, very few produce one. Monthly newsletters can broadcast news, interesting tidbits, and information related to an industry. If you also invite the audience to take advantage of a special offer, refer a friend for a discount, or benefit from a holiday deal, the response rates are higher. Emails can also be automated and used for appointment follow-up, appointment reminders, birthday greetings, or to reach clients that have not visited the practice in six months or more. Businesses struggle with using email effectively, and most owners think the challenge is generating good content. They're focusing on the wrong problem. The real challenge is developing a robust, ever- growing email marketing list.

If your practice hasn't used email previously, chances are the list is outdated and much smaller than it should be. Every single contact with a potential or existing patient represents business income. Let's say a new patient is worth $5,000 in the course of one year. Maybe that's a big number but, as an example sake, let's run with it. If you understood that sending someone a letter, they would respond by sending you a $5,000 check, would you find time to write that letter? And, if sending 20 letters meant receiving $100,000, would you find the time?

That's basically what email campaigns are about. You can engage, draw in, and build a foundation of people who become new patients. You can also keep existing patients close to the business. A person interested enough in the services you provide, someone willing to fill out a form and submit their contact information, is one of the most valuable assets a practice can have. So, why do so many businesses fail to gather this information and build lists? That's one of the very few questions I don't have an answer for.

A business should be equipped to collect four essential pieces of information from anyone who comes to them through an online platform: their first name, last name, email address, and phone number. Nothing is more critical to the success of practice than implementing a system that builds a growing contact list. An ever-expanding email list = a growing practice.

Very few practices do this, by the way, even though it can contribute to an effortless boost in new patient appointments, often as much as 25% every month. Why not? Although it is impossible to go back in time and find the people a practice has lost touch with, it is possible to adopt a new philosophy moving forward. Understand that every point of contact with a new person matters from now on. This is practical advice. What if you want to change your office policy? What if there is an emergency and you have to shut down for a time? What if you bring on a new staff member? Someone who has followed the advice can quickly communicate with everyone associated with their practice by crafting a message and hitting a button. Emails can be used to share forms in advance of an office visit, send an unexpected cancellation, or to solicit positive reviews. Having an up-to-date contact list even makes it easier to create and push out content to other social media platforms. What are you waiting for?

Email marketing is one of the easiest, most effective tools out there.

Content Marketing

A practice is only as good as its online content. Plenty of owners would like to reject that theory, but it's not an overstatement. As it has been stated before in this book, over 97% of people seeking a service do online research about it. NINETY-SEVEN PERCENT. That's the audience you are missing out on if you don't take care of your online content.

This is a vast network, full of potential new patients. But, there is very little time to capture their attention. People tend to make snap judgments about what they see online. Do they want to know more? Are you the real deal? What specifically do you offer, and will it help them? That's what they want to know. Every original, well-written blog post, every meaningful Facebook post, every authentic video has the potential to win an audience over. Good content elicits a sense of trust, belonging, status, and in the case of weight loss, determination and inspiration.

That is the primary job of any weight loss practitioner anyway, encouraging, inspiring, and supporting people so that they can finally lose weight. Lively blog posts, new strategies, studies, recipes, patient success stories; all can be used on the website and social media platforms to win new patients. This element of digital marketing should include video testimonials from patients. These are not polished commercials, just real people telling a real story about how the practice helped them to lose weight. There is no better way to build trust than to show people someone that seems familiar to them, like a neighbor or a friend, not a supermodel or stock photo.

There is a lesser-known method of generating traffic, known as the press release. This is a news release that goes to distribution sites, gets categorized, and sent to hundreds of smaller, more local sites. The biggest news distribution organizations (AP Newwire, Google News, Newswire Today) serve as feeder sites. Local news channels use these larger sites to troll for interesting pieces for their local platform. When something new happens at a practice, they win a local business award, they hire a new practitioner or open a new location, it's news. It can be used to get attention and a higher ranking.

General content that is not weight loss specific is also important. If a practice focuses only on themselves, all the time, people start to perceive it as advertising, and they move on. Give them a great headline and fascinating new information about weight loss, health, fitness, nutrition, creating a weight loss mindset - and a practice can capture a whole new audience. This may sound like a lot of work, and it can be, but a systemized, automated approach can make this relatively easy.

Putting out content related to the local community is also a great way to earn attention. Earlier in the book, we discussed how important it is to be seen as a genuine, caring business that serves people well and is a valuable member of the community. Being covered by a local news entity using press releases is an approach we recommend.

Search Results

Traffic that comes to a website from search engines (i.e., because the business has a higher ranking in search results) isn't as valuable as many marketers will tell you it is. Marketing teams don't often talk about how many calls a practice is getting, because they aren't generating that kind of result. They are merely reporting how many people they get to visit your site. If it's not qualified traffic, and if the site isn't set up right, it won't help.

This is one of the most widely misunderstood myths about marketing on the Internet in the history of digital marketing. SEO, as a stand-alone strategy, is prohibitively expensive. It is extremely difficult to create and maintain a strategy that continually brings in new business. This is true especially if the business is attempting to do it in-house.

When "search engine optimization" is done right, it supports an overall big picture strategy. Many, many practices have been led down this path, throwing money at SEO services with no real plan. I would love to tell you that being #1 in your market for the #1 search phrase in your industry automatically results in a rush of new patients. But, it simply isn't true. There are practices that rank at the top of their service area who still struggle to get new patients. The top spots are not always the most lucrative.

Fun Fact; you can dramatically change a practice without needing to compete for the #1 spot using the most popular keywords in the industry. That much IS true.

Growing a weight loss practice means investing substantially and consistently in a market. But, it must be an investment that covers a lot of ground, a big picture strategy that utilizes all of the approaches outlined in this guide, all working together. This is how a practice wins new weight loss patients consistently. The main thing is to keep all of these efforts results-driven, with analytics that can be tracked; the only metric that matters is how many new patients you end up seeing. That's how a practice succeeds and grows.

Pay Per Click

Throwing good money after a bad is not a winning strategy, and yet, many practice owners do just that. They continue with expensive paid ads, Ad word campaigns, or other pay-to-play services, without a knowledgeable person managing the effort. As their pay-per-click costs soar, the new patient flow isn't large enough to cover the costs, let alone show a profit. If this sounds familiar, fear not. It's a very common occurrence.

One painful truth; paid traffic is a necessary part of the plan. It has to be. Clients must invest something to increase their reach and find the right kind of traffic, people specifically interested in weight loss services. But, the better news? It doesn't have to be prohibitively expensive.

The main things to remember about pay-per-click traffic are:

Ad campaigns must be created and managed by someone who knows what they are doing. A lot of in-house teams use a "spray and pray" method. They blindly throw money at platforms like Facebook or pay to promote offers on Twitter, without identifying a specific audience. Then, they don't get results. The only ones to make money in this scenario are Facebook, Twitter, and Google!

The creation and distribution of pay-per-click ads must be continuously monitored and assessed using sophisticated analytics. This is how you build a process for finding new patients that is repeatable and scalable. This way, you can always get more new patients at a lower cost.

Paid ad campaigns must be monitored, cared for, and updated daily, weekly, monthly. That is a cold, hard truth, but we have to give it to you straight. It takes time, knowledge, and analytics to keep things running. This does require an investment, but the good news is, the right approach will quickly pay for itself.

If you receive a proposal from a marketing group, and it seems outrageously low, ask about their "new business metrics." Not traffic. Tell them you want to know how they track new patient phone calls and office visits. If you think the service is cheap, expect to "get what you paid for," which is very little. Conversely, if the costs seem incredibly high, ask what their metrics are, and if it includes measuring new business income.

The right mindset about pay-per-click is to establish the cost of acquiring a new patient and comparing that with the income it represents. Then, measure how many new people come through every month. The overall pay-per-click plan must be profitable and maintained over time. If a pay-per-click effort isn't done right, it can turn into an expensive nightmare.

However, pay-per-click campaigns launched as part of a broader, more comprehensive strategy can turn a practice around. We've seen it happen.

Really, what matters most is the person doing the clicking. How close are they to deciding on visiting a weight loss clinic? Are they ready to make the call? Identifying who has a certain mindset, getting them on your list, and consistently communicating until they become a new patient requires some paid traffic. But, it's traffic that pays off.

That's really the crux of all of this. Pay someone 10K or a hundred K, and watch as they create nice Facebook posts, get new followers on IG, or publish a fun video of your dog on twitter that gets hundreds of reshares, and it's all good. Until you realize you aren't getting any more new patients or an increase in income. Now it's just become another business expense.

The idea that a big-picture marketing strategy must drive toward a single business goal isn't discussed in weight loss marketing. Why is that?

The answer is simple. It is hard to do.

In the end, the most important thing to remember is this: Transforming a weight loss practice into a thriving, growing business that enjoys a good reputation, ever-increasing profits, and a valuable place in the community is what it's all about. And, those things are directly tied to how much the practice invests...in staff, in customer service, in providing services that people need. But also in a strong digital marketing plan.

Get Access To A Professional Design Team That Will Create A Free Banner For You ($499 Value): http://weight-loss-traffic.com

Chapter 10: Automation

Achieving Marketing Efficiency Through Automation

As you read through this book, it will become apparent that launching a successful online marketing strategy is a lot of hard and very detailed work. Anything worth doing always is. One of the advantages of online marketing is that some tasks can be automated. We've seen clients commit to going without it, and I admire their spunk. But churning out content on various platforms, linking it all together, responding to inquiries, list building, and the constant analysis is overwhelming. In-house marketing quickly becomes someone's full-time job, or it takes valuable time away from your schedule, the time you could spend treating patients.

It's important to make the distinction between a marketing expert and someone that likes being on Facebook. Digital marketing has been around for decades. Large tech firms like Google and Facebook are massive companies out to monetize their platforms. You must acquire excellent technical skills to use them as effective marketing tools. Understanding in-depth how they work is how you make money, not just spend it.

It's not easy to manage a sophisticated strategy in-house. There is the cost of a staff person, social accounts to open and optimize, software to purchase and install, subscription fees, continual content creation. And, who will track all of the calls and enter in new customer data? Who will manage your growing contact lists? Follow-up is a vital component of any Internet marketing effort. It has to be immediate and meaningful, but who is going to do that for you? DIY marketing takes time, financial resources, expertise, and laser focus on business growth. Is there anyone in your practice who has the know-how and time to do this well?

As more and more patients call and make appointments, the more challenging it will be to keep up with marketing efforts. Your DIY marketing person will likely get caught up in managing new patients or drawn into handling administrative responsibilities. They begin to put off essential marketing tasks for "another day." Of course, that day never comes. Before long, the marketing tasks grind to a halt, and eventually, the new patient flow wanes. That's what you want to avoid at all costs.

Hiring a reputable, experienced team is the best option. Outsourcing frees you up to continue focusing on running and growing your practice. But, if you still feel you want to take the in-house route, automated systems can help.

Automated systems can track web traffic, register new contacts, generate autoresponder messages, push social content out, and schedule follow-up messages for potential new clients. You can scale up as things get busier and more profitable. One thing I can tell you with certainty is that the marketing engine must keep running! One more reason to recommend automation.

A Follow-up Framework

Before we talk about the framework, let me answer a commonly asked question: What do we mean by follow up? Well, simply put, when you put out lots of relevant content, it generates online traffic to your website. People find your content and follow the links to your site. We're not talking about people who come through the door, that's called foot traffic. We're talking about what happens when someone finds you online and visits your website. When they visit, they might submit an "interest form" or call or email your practice. When they do, what is your response?

I can't tell you how often during the exploratory phase with a possible new client, they reveal to me that they have no follow-up plan. Because their previous attempts at marketing failed to bring in new leads, they've never had to consider how they would follow-up. They aren't ready for an influx of new patient phone calls or new leads!

It's a sorry state of affairs when marketing efforts are so feeble that nothing happens. When we implement our program for clients, things do happen. But, there's nothing more frustrating than when they aren't ready. Any new person that visits your website is hard-earned. Every new phone call is valuable, and there is a dollar amount attached to every lead. That's the hard truth about digital marketing.

There is a vast online world out there with millions of paths people can follow to find what they are looking for. When the path they choose leads to your website and ultimately your practice, you had better be ready. They are about to entrust you with personal information, name, phone number, and email address. More importantly, they are about to trust you with their dream of losing weight and getting healthier. They deserve to be treated with warmth and respect. This begins with timely, professional follow-ups.

Funnel Vision

As a practice grows, it becomes more challenging to follow up with people who express interest in your services. There are ways to build automated systems, called sales "funnels," that make the process easier. Every single person that visits your website and fills out the contact form should go into this funnel. Once they do, they become a "warm," lead. The contact form on your site, or social media accounts is a port of entry for new contacts. This is how you capture information and find creative ways to communicate with them further. Of course, as they progress through the funnel, there is one goal; convert them into new patients.

My team works hard to deliver highly qualified prospects to our clients, and this type of funnel is integral to our success and theirs. As a list grows over time, an automated system becomes even more critical. Smart practitioners understand that a clean, growing contact list is a mission-critical asset. You invest a lot in getting people to discover your practice and pay attention. Letting things fall apart after they sign up makes no sense. Anyone interested enough in your weight loss services, who clicks through to your website and submits their personal information, deserves a timely, welcoming response and a continuing digital dialogue. There are no exceptions to this rule.

An automated funnel allows a practice to create and schedule engaging and informative messages to warm leads, and capture data on new ones. This keeps your clinic at the top of people's minds until they are ready to call for that first appointment. Automated systems make this far more efficient than it would be otherwise.

The system we use for our clients is called an "autoresponder." It's a system set up to accomplish many goals. First, it alerts us when someone new has submitted their information. Second, we use it to create and schedule professional messages in a more personal way. There are many different ways to go about it, and we can talk through that in a bit. But for now, just know that autoresponders can be programmed to send a series of texts, emails, or calls (straight to voicemail). For example, a typical autoresponder email looks something like this:

A warm lead should hear from you as soon as they submit their contact information. Many companies have developed software that handles these kinds of tasks. No matter which system you choose to purchase and implement, it must capture names and store customer data in an organized way. This "capture" aspect is key to setting up an efficient, automated response process. The system should also have a feature that captures phone numbers. Keep in mind that this is NOT so that you can begin robocalling potential new clients to death! The goal is to email them and set up a reasonable sequence of communications. Once they become patients, phone calls or texts will be appropriate, so think ahead and collect their information.

Autoresponder and Customer Management Systems (CMS) can even be set-up to alert a designated person in your office to let them know you've heard from a new patient. The alert might look something like this: "Congratulations! [NAME] has just left a message and is interested in scheduling an appointment. Here is their email address and phone number." Another advantage of automation is that the Internet never sleeps! A system that works 24/7 to receive new contact names and respond instantly is a terrific benefit. This around-the-clock capability is powerful. You never risk losing a potential new patient just because they've tried to reach you outside of office hours. Thanks to today's technology, your practice is always "open" and available to follow-up with more information.

It happens all the time. Patients are browsing in the middle of the night, and they make a snap decision to reach out. Imagine if they immediately get a nice email with information and encouragement that, with your help, they can lose weight! Even a brief "Thank you for reaching out, we'll be in touch soon," is enough. Later, you can follow-up with them by calling, sending them your newsletter, or texting them a link to a patient success story or a special offer.

Pro tip: The longer you wait to follow up, the less likely your warm lead will convert to a new patient.

Studies show that warm leads cool off quickly. Make sure your autoresponder is up and running perfectly, and your staff is trained. Coaching can help, so can a staff script. They should answer the phone with one goal only, book an appointment. When returning calls or reaching out to a warm lead, they can say, "Hi! This is [NAME] from [PRACTICE]. I see that you called our practice last week to schedule an appointment. I'm calling to see if you have any questions and when would be a good time for you to come in." Chances are, they will! This kind of communication and system is highly effective.

Personal, professional follow-up with potential new patients is one of the best marketing practices I can recommend. And, your competitors probably aren't doing it. The bigger and bolder that first step is, the better. Send an automated email, followed by a useful report on weight loss strategies. Follow that up with a new patient offer. All of this leads the patient further into the funnel and closer to believing that you are a practitioner they can trust. This engagement is how warm leads become new patients. Quite often, it takes more than just answering the phone.

More + More = New Business

In this day in age, when we are all on information overload, one attempt to reach out isn't enough. Email several times. People are used to it! Now that most people are accessing all kinds of information on their phones, they're less likely to respond the first time you contact them. And, hiding behind emails isn't personal enough. Real person-to-person communication must be a part of your funnel.

When we build a funnel for clients, we create an entire series of emails, texts, and call scripts. We schedule precise, targeted communications and tweak them based on the analytics. The series begins with a request for contact information and an offer of a free report. It ends with a script and coaching for those answering the phone, to ensure that every patient interaction is personal and professional, and results in a booked appointment. We create newsletter templates so you can share patient success stories, local news, and special offers. This helps you maintain a strong patient base and loops in new patients.

The practice you are building is not an e-commerce business where people anonymously, impulsively purchase products. Weight loss is a service business, and that means warm leads need cultivation and encouragement. It is about developing an online rapport through a mix of automated and more personal interactions essential. When it comes to weight loss, there's no shopping cart; no impulse buys, no button to push for immediate gratification. Instead, this is a decision that gets made over time. People have deeply ingrained habits that need breaking or a fear of failure. It's challenging for new contacts to trust you enough to make that first call. Help them by using an automated funnel to stay in touch and remain encouraging.

Does this require legwork? Absolutely. Does it result in new business? In our experience, absolutely, YES. And we have the data to prove it.

So, set up an automated communications that will act as a personalized connector to new leads and work to earn their trust. By putting in a sincere effort, new leads will become new patients and fuel the growth of your practice.

Pro Tip: Include a link to your contact form in your blog posts, newsletters, and social media posts.

Your autoresponder system can accept contact information from sources other than your web site. You can create and load up "broadcast messages" each month and integrate activity with your contact database. Contacts that continue to subscribe to your email list are open to hearing from you and are more likely to become patients. Don't neglect them!

Patience & Persistence Wins

Effective online marketing involves holding a long-term view. Potential new patients might not be ready to commit. They may be tentative about addressing their weight loss issues because it's been challenging for them. Once they find your content, visit your website, and start hearing from you, timing is everything. Perhaps they've failed in the past, or they lack the proper knowledge. Whatever the issue, if you continue to offer encouragement, information, and support, you'll win them over.

Periodic, professional, and personal. These are the Three P's that draw new people into your practice using an automated marketing and communications funnel. In marketing terms, it's called "top-of-mind aware-ness." Stay in their thoughts by showing up regularly in their inbox, popping (sparingly) into their text messages, leave a friendly voice mail, and before long; they will make that call to your office to schedule an appointment.

Just The Facts:

– Follow-up is crucial, but it's equally important that the process is automated: no one should be sending out newsletters or follow-ups by hand, nor adding anyone manually to a list. At the same time, don't just follow-up with your leads via technology. You can ask the office staff to follow-up as well. Have an employee call the lead back as soon as possible, while they're still interested. Show potential new patients that your practice is professional, yet personal and ready to do business.

– It's essential to keep regular contact with your patients: fire off a blog post once a month to your email lists, and keep your business at the top of their minds.

Chapter 11: ROI and the Bottom Line

How To Make More Than You Spend

Traditional advertising strategies cost far more than online solutions, and the results are questionable. This is true, partly because the metrics for TV, print ads, or radio spots are hard to track. Agencies may have data on the potential for an audience, but that's about it. Usually, clients come to us after they've invested in traditional tactics, like buying ads in the Yellow Pages Directory, purchasing expensive spots on radio or TV, or participating in programs with ZocDoc, Groupon or Yelp. Sometimes these decisions are made at the recommendation of an account rep. In other cases, it's the suggestion of someone in-house, a social media staffer who hasn't done their research. In both cases, pay-to-play advertising has gobbled up significant working capital and a substantial chunk of their small business budget without bringing in new patients.

When we consult with any new client, the discussion starts with asking about their marketing history. Chances are they've paid fees to at least one service provider without seeing an uptick in new business. Often, they have a staff person interested in SEO that they pay to dabble in "marketing." In these early meetings, we ask some pretty tough questions. We find out about marketing investments they've made in the past and the results of those efforts. When we ask about traffic stats and new patient calls, things start to get uncomfortable. No one wants to admit that the marketing decisions they've made in the past didn't lead to a more profitable future. Please know that this is very common, and if it sounds familiar, you are not alone. The truth is if you've made a significant investment in an ad agency or you have a top-notch staff person, and your marketing brings in significant new business, you don't need us. And that's great! You can stop reading right here.

If, however, your new patient flow is minimal, or your practice isn't as profitable as you would like, there's still hope. We've seen the damage done by those promising that "SEO," or a directory listing will save the day. Not all marketing consultants are sharks. Some of them have your best interests at heart; they just lack the expertise or experience to bring new business into your practice and make it profitable. But after paying for several months, or a year, and getting no new patient calls, what's next? Convince yourself that online marketing doesn't work? Shift from one low-cost, superficial tactic to another? There is a far better way, one that is results-driven with increasing patient calls every month.

My team is about one thing: business growth. I can't grow my business unless I grow yours. At first, that might mean sharing some painful truths with you, including identifying the approaches that aren't working, and why.

A well planned, robust strategy, like the one outlined here, is what's needed. Online marketing, when done well, offers enormous advantages over traditional methods. Online marketing can be results-driven, and deliver solid metrics of success. Comprehensive online strategies require more than posting on Facebook, putting shots on Instagram, or sending out an email now and then. This program is a sophisticated, detailed engine with many parts. Each aspect of this step-by-step plan feeds into one goal, a constant increase in calls from new patients, gains you can track. And, in the end, it costs less than TV, radio or billboards.

We start at the very core of your business and build out from there. We'll help you develop an online presence that works 24/7 to reach thousands of new people who demonstrate by their online activity that they are interested in losing weight. We'll show you how to improve your ranking, get five-star reviews, and create an online presence that leads people to act.

Our singular goal is to help potential new patients find you, believe in you and call your office for an appointment. We are unique in that analytics are built into everything that we do, including new patient call reports. We capture data about who is visiting your website and how they got there. We track your rise in the rankings, your conversion rates, and we analyze the cost for each new patient. There are even metrics for how effective your online content is. There are ways to track how many conversions you get per month, people who move from being in the "sales funnel" to signing on as a new patient. Every month, you'll get a report detailing the new calls coming into your practice. If your marketing team is not providing this metric, you are not really tracking the success of your marketing, and your investment of time and money may be in vain.

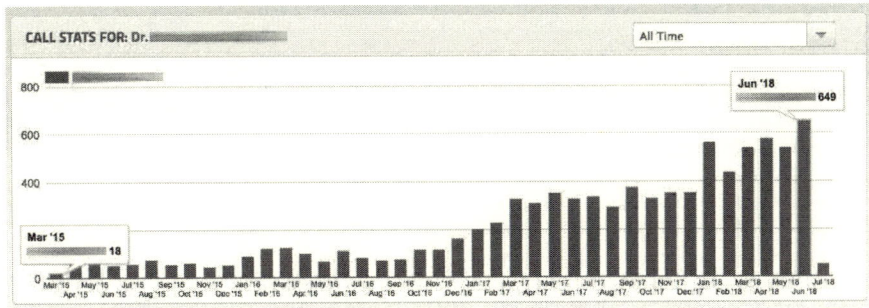

Call Tracking and Analytics

Tracking and Analytics

Tracking marketing results means understanding the cost of getting a new patient versus the profit value of that new patient over the long term. That's what we're about, that all-important metric. If it costs you more to market than what those efforts represent in terms of new business, obviously something needs to change. The solution is a smart marketing strategy, one that includes real-time data and analytics. It's all about how you use the tools and integrate metrics into the process.

Partial data like how many people have subscribed to your social media channel or the number of tweets that went out are not results-driven numbers. The real story is how many people follow through to visit your website and call your office to schedule an appointment. We don't settle for any other metric, and neither should you. How many people call your practice to schedule weight loss appointments, and what happens when they do is the key to the success of your clinic.

This topic alone could be an entire book all by itself. Many weight loss practice owners think that they know what takes place every day when new patients call their practice. The truth is that most doctors are shocked to learn what is happening (or not happening) when calls come into their practice.

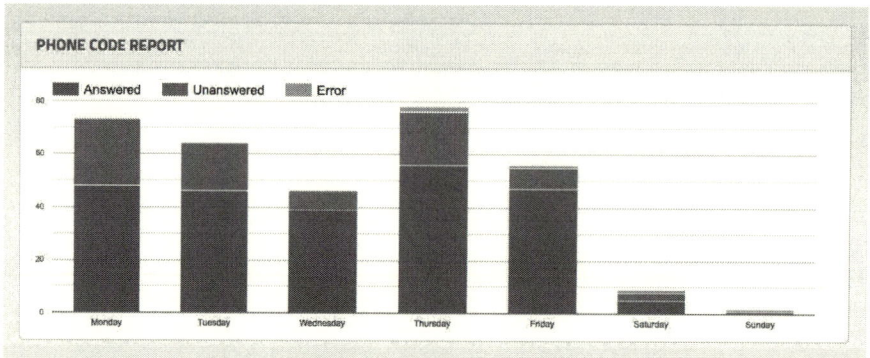

Inbound Call Reporting for Missed Calls

If new patient calls are not handled well, if people call with questions or want to schedule an appointment, but don't have a pleasant experience, the marketing won't matter. It sounds obvious, yet the majority of weight loss practices that contact us for help are missing tremendous opportunities by not approaching their inbound call process efficiently. I'll say it another way. Call management and customer service is the key to turning a practice around. It's not the search results, social media posts, pay-per-click, or anything else. Define this process. Hire the right people to answer your phone and train them well. Consider the cost to get new patients to call your practice and then ask yourself why you would risk losing or mismanaging those calls. A clinic spends hundreds of dollars getting new people to call but then doesn't care about converting them into new patients? It doesn't make any sense.

Pro Tip: You can track the keywords people are using to find you. Your Google My Business page has data on who has visited and how they got there.

A Word About Google Analytics

There are ways to assess your ranking. But, all of those numbers must add up to one thing-an increase in new patient calls. Some local directory sites offer tracking tools; however, the dominant player in tracking and metrics is Google Analytics. These tools are the most beneficial aspect of the radical approach called online marketing.

Google Analytics is an absolute must-have. If it's not in use on your website, ask your webmaster to set it up. That's how vital Google Analytics is to your ROI (Return on Investment). It tells you who's visiting, who's clicking, what data they're entering, how well your website is converting visitors into leads. It allows you to assess how long potential new patients stay on your website, and more.

Google Analytics is an essential tool for monitoring your ROI and website traffic, another critical task. And probably one that a busy medical practitioner doesn't have the time or capacity to manage. My guess is you are not an online marketing geek that understands metrics on a deep level. Tracking website hits and phone calls from new patients is incredibly important (you deserve to know if your marketing plan is working). But, we've found that most practitioners are too busy taking care of patients to be an analytics guru, as it should be. So, we provide great analytics for our private clients. They hire us to implement their online marketing systems and processes, and we make sure to track web traffic and conversion rates. Plus, we send a detailed report every month.

Pro Tip: When placing ads on any platform, use a different phone number. You are probably thinking, "SAY WHAT?" The idea of not using a primary office phone number when marketing a practice online seems counterintuitive. But, phone numbers don't matter as much as they used to. People tap a button to dial these days; no one looks at numbers anymore. So, we create unique identifier numbers for marketing offers and forward those calls to your regular number. This doesn't register with the patient; they're mostly unaware of the number they're using to reach you. A unique phone number makes it possible to track where the calls are coming from and what efforts bring in the best results.

We recommend creating unique phone numbers for every marketing ad or campaign and forwarding the calls to your practice. This way, you can know with certainty which online ads and campaigns trigger calls from new patients. You can see how many calls each unique number has received, and what content inspired the click-through. Now, you'll know what works and what needs tweaking, which is ROI gold!

You don't have to get rid of your current phone number; you shouldn't. By using what we call a "unique identifier," communications can be analyzed for their effectiveness. Any marketing firm not using metrics does not want its success rate tracked. This is not a good sign that they are working to grow your practice.

A Tracking Toolkit

There is a great toolkit called Google Webmaster Tools. This feature tells you how many people link to your account or site all across the Internet so you can assess how well your online strategy is working. Data can be added, statistics that exist in your email platform, as well. You can tell how many potential new patients are in your "funnel," how many autoresponders have gone out, how many people have opened and read your email, and more. When you compare this data with the number of contacts that have called your office, you know exactly where you stand and why.

Another opportunity to track results is built into internal CRM (Customer Relationship Management) systems. Some practitioners set up and use their CRMs to track how much they make per patient visit versus the time spent with each patient to assess profitability. We will cover this topic in more detail later on. For now, just know that some key metrics will help determine your Marketing Return On Investment.

Assuming that you already have a CRM in place, explore the built-in analytics it offers. If you don't have a CRM, get one. It's a critical tool for any business, an efficient way to organize and reach existing patients and stay in touch with potential new patients. Selecting the right CRM, and learning how to use it is beyond the scope of this book. However, be sure to choose wisely. Some of the contact management tools out there are too sophisticated, and it will be costly to manage in-house and impossible to use. Too simple, and you won't be able to automate specific processes and ease the workload. With the right set up, you can develop automated marketing and business processes, become more efficient, and engage with and convert new clients.

There is an unlimited number of ways to track marketing efforts. Some of them are more important than others. The key to growing a practice rests entirely on three things: the number of phone calls from new patients who found you online, how the calls are handled, and what it cost to get the call. These are the metrics that matter.

A Case for Working with Us

When we meet with new clients to discuss the parameters of working together, they often tell us they have a marketing plan. And, they believe that they do. But, dig deeper, and typically we find that pieces are missing. Our first step is to show them how results-driven marketing, tracking, and profitability works. When they see our case studies backed up by data, including new call reports, they're on board.

Potential new clients typically reach out after they've spent time and money on marketing without seeing any increase in new patient calls. This is frustrating for me. As an online marketing professional with over two decades of experience, I believe they deserve better. YOU deserve better.

My job is to develop an Internet marketing strategy with achievable goals for business growth, and then work diligently to reach them. Most importantly, we do it all for substantially less than a full-time staff person or big agency.

Pro Tip: Please don't accept anything less than a comprehensive marketing strategy with built-in analytics and achievable goals for profitability. You deserve it.

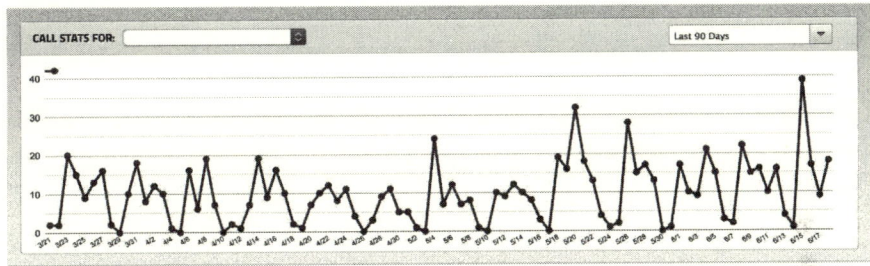

90 Day Inbound Call Reporting and Tracking

Here is an example of the part of our monthly reporting:

Monthly Call Tracking & REPORTING

EAST SIDE OFFICE

Date Range:	1/1/2020 To 1/31/2020
Total Calls:	540
New Patient	183 (33.88%)
Returning Patient	97 (17.96%)
Missed Call	119 (22.03%)
Cost Per New Patient:	

WEST SIDE OFFICE

Date Range:	1/1/2020 To 1/31/2020
Total Calls:	386
New Patient	120 (31.08%)
Returning Patient	68 (17.61%)
Missed Call	77 (19.94%)
Cost Per New Patient:	

It is crucial to help clients assess the value of each new patient. A new visitor to your office represents an income average. Let's say you spent $36,000 on marketing efforts for one year. You determine that 1,200 unique patients came through those online pathways. You can now assess the average number of visits a patient typically makes and understand the value of that one new patient. You can expect to get additional referrals from a new patient, which increases their worth to your practice. Compare these numbers with any new patients who hear about you through other channels, and you'll see that online efforts are a lucrative investment. This is how actual business growth works. These metrics may seem basic, and yet, most practitioners neglect to employ analytics to measure profitability and growth.

My goal is to ensure that every client has a specific plan for how the marketing strategy we create and launch for them will be tracked. We offer an accurate assessment of new client valuation. When you understand how many people you have drawn in thanks to paid and unpaid online marketing platforms and services, you'll know with certainty that you have a successful plan. You will always know how to get more patients and how much it will cost you to do so. This is true whether you hire my team, or work internally following the strategies we've laid out here.

It's distressing how often we face the challenge of building a whole new online marketing infrastructure for a client, after they have paid an enormous amount of money to an agency or several independent consultants, without seeing results. Together, my clients and I decide ahead of time what metrics will be most useful. This is always the number of inbound patient calls. Then, we design, build and launch the strategy necessary to deliver those results. We know before we set out what success looks like for your practice. Any marketing team you work with should approach it this way, even if your team is in-house.

I can't stress this point enough. You need to be thinking about your ROI, the return on your online marketing investments, AT ALL TIMES. Efficient and accurate monitoring of online efforts will give you peace of mind and an unparalleled advantage over traditional media and your competitors. Wouldn't you like to know, down to the dollar, whether spending money in the online arena to get new patients is a good investment? I do. It's what drives me to work hard on behalf of my clients every day. I encourage all of my clients to pursue this information, letting them know that if they do not see at least three times their marketing investment in new business, something needs to change.

This guide is meant to help you create and manage an internal marketing strategy. However, let me also say this: If the revenue generated from your marketing is less than what you've spent after six months, it's probably time to call in an expert. Often it's clear after a few months if anything is working. Do not be led astray by the idea that improved search results are the only metric of value. Success is seen in the number of new calls you receive each month. It's not your fault that you don't fully grasp the complexity that is online marketing. There are markets and geographic areas where it's hard to get traction. Or maybe you're missing a few steps in the process, or the messaging is off. In any case, bringing in a professional who can devise, implement effective strategies is money well spent, because it results in new business and increased profits. We can help you finally crack the code and achieve marketing success.

Even if you are resistant to hiring my team, consider how you will track the marketing person or agency you do hire. You must know how to determine whether their efforts are working in your best interest.

Pro Tip: If you work with an agency and they don't offer ROI reports, ask! If they refuse, something isn't right. If they refuse, something isn't right. They might be hiding poor statistics, or they're not as good as they say they are.

There is power in identifying the marketing dollars spent, and whether they result in phone calls from new patients. The more control you have over this kind of information, the more valuable your online marketing strategy will be.

Our job is to bring new weight loss patients into your practice. Your task is to serve them well and help them get healthier by losing weight. Once this happens, they'll give you an excellent review, tell their friends, family, and co-workers, and soon more new patients will arrive. Your ranking will get higher and higher, and before long, your practice will dominate the search results in your market. It's quite extraordinary; the potential online marketing has for exponential growth. What are you waiting for?

Just The Facts:

– ROI tracking on print and TV ads is scarce and ineffectual at best: online ROI tracking offers a wealth of information and enables you to very precisely track your marketing.

– You must have a stable, well-defined system to correctly track your ROI. Know where your money is going and what percentage of leads you're converting! If you work with a marketing agency, they must provide ROI numbers. If they don't have them or don't want you to see them, something is seriously wrong.

Chapter 12: Where To Go From Here

Keeping Up With the Trends

Because you've read this guide through to this chapter, pat yourself on the back! You have now done more to develop an online marketing strategy than most weight loss practitioners. By creating a plan and implementing the steps outlined in this book, you've got a solid foundation laid out for pulling in new patients from the worldwide web.

That means:
You see your practice ranking highly for specific keyword search terms,
You've got a dedicated website with a strong call to action,
You're leveraging the power of Facebook, and you're a Twitter regular!
You've got a sophisticated system of follow-ups,
You've got ROI tracking methods, and you can pinpoint your highest-profit channels with incredible accuracy.
And, you can repeat the process based on how much you spend!

Bravo!

But, hold on.

When it comes to marketing and Internet technology, the number one thing to remember is that you can never become complacent. The rules change constantly. The Internet is, by its very nature, a vast landscape of opportunity. Google and search engines will always tweak their algorithms and develop new services to give their users the best experience. New platforms will launch. Facebook and other channels will add new features to grow their advertising revenue from business owners like you. You've got to stay informed and thoughtful.

As a small and responsive team, we are committed to staying on top of every single development in the world of online marketing, SEO, reputation, call flow, and profitability. Our expertise allows us to tweak marketing strategies for clients to leverage the newest trends and drop anything that becomes ineffective.

Many Internet developments are brewing right now, innovations and changes that will impact online marketing soon. There are up and coming tech companies, new tools, and ever-changing human behavior. We'll help you keep an eye on your business while peering into the future to prepare for upcoming trends. With that in mind, here are some upcoming trends:

Mobile

The increasing use of mobile devices is perhaps the most urgent of all challenges that Internet marketers face. The use of mobile devices as the primary vehicle of interaction with the Internet is increasing rapidly. One recent study asserts that the number of website visits using mobile devices in 2018 rose from 57% to 63%. The exploration of websites with mobile devices increased from 40% to 49% in one year. In November of 2016, StatCounter released figures that, for the first time, showed that more people are accessing the Internet using a mobile device than are accessing the Internet using a PC. Mobile devices now account for over 51.3% of all Internet access traffic.

This increase is a driving force behind many of the search engine developments coming up. Google set up its Local Places infrastructure primarily because search information is now being accessed more often through mobile devices. What does that mean for your practice? A mobile search is entirely different from traditional computer or laptop searches. Research has shown that those using mobile devices search with more urgency. Users are impatient and searching in ways that state, "I need something right now, and I want it to be nearby." We refer to this as the "proximity" principle. This is primarily true of service-oriented businesses. Searchers are willing to sift through Google search results to find what they are looking for locally. The data demonstrates that people are looking for easy access and personalized service close to home and or work. And they like to act quickly. This is terrific news for medical weight loss practices.

Thousands of your prospective new patients are at work, out shopping, relaxing, getting coffee, and all the while they are scrolling through information on their phones. You can put your service information out there for them to see. If losing weight is anywhere near the top of their list of life concerns, we'd like to know that they'll see content from you, not your competitor. I hope it's you and your practice that gets their phone call.

Many of our new clients are skeptical at first. Once they see the new patient flow and hear people say they found them online, it restores their belief. Digital marketing, done well, does work.

Pro Tip: Your website must be mobile-friendly, formatted to show up perfectly on any device.

As the use of mobile devices increases, it is of critical importance that your site is mobile-friendly. All of the images and content must be formatted to be "mobile-responsive." Your website has to look great and function flawlessly on any mobile device, with images correctly sized and formatted. Same for your blog, newsletters are any other social content.

Get Social

We've covered a great deal of information regarding social media platforms and accounts. Hopefully, you can learn to navigate social networks with effective marketing. Now, let's talk about the future of social networks, how they're going to change, and how they will impact online marketing strategies.

The most important clue to the future of social platforms is understanding how they are evolving into more than places to connect with others, or consume content. Social media networks are turning into search engine tools. People are using platforms like Facebook and Twitter, not just to interact but to conduct Internet searches. They want information, reviews, and suggestions, and their preferred social network will be what they use to find answers. People will increasingly search using their preferred social platforms instead of using Google or other tools. What does this mean for your practice? It means now, more than ever, there should be a sense of urgency about establishing a substantial online presence for your practice and keeping up with the latest changes. It also means keeping on top of the preferred platforms of your target audience.

Even if you've done little to improve your rankings or build an online presence, it's not too late! You are not behind the curve yet. If you start now and create a significant presence on sites like LinkedIn, Twitter, Facebook, YouTube, StumbleUpon, Digg, and others, you'll be in an excellent position to grow your business.

I'm not saying you have to interact with every social media network and channel. Nor do you have to be active on these platforms all the time, or every day. That's impossible. What it does mean, however, is that you must be a solid frontrunner, a noticeable presence on the platforms where your potential new patients spend time. To do that, you need far more than a website and a few local directory listings.

Local Focus

Social networks are getting more location-minded, just like Google. We expect this trend to continue. I predict this will eventually lead to a social-mobile combo, a one-two punch. Users will be searching using Google or other search engine tools alongside their Facebook mobile app, or the apps related to their platforms of choice. We already see this pattern of usage. Facebook is expanding its platform with search features, developing a Places feature, and a Facebook Local option. They are poised to become the next big search engine platform, opening opportunities for local marketers and smaller businesses.

Based on the data regarding search behavior and the sheer number of Facebook users worldwide, you'll want to be in local search results for these platforms. Invest where you know your ideal audience is spending time and where potential new weight loss clients are active. The good thing about this focus on "local" is that you can be seen more readily and easily if your online marketing plan is implemented correctly.

Ranking Rights & Referrals

If you don't have a Google My Business page (which is mobile-friendly), you'll miss out on about 60% of the hordes of people searching on the Internet for your services. The growth of mobile use has also tightened up ranking requirements. What does that mean? On a regular desktop with a larger screen, you can show up as one of the top 7 in rankings. When it comes to mobile devices and their small screens, you have to be in the top 3 to 5 spots to get the best result.

Few people scroll very far down a list of search returns. It's far more likely that you will earn a click-through or call if you are in the first few listings. Mobile phones offer unparalleled ease of use and almost constant access to potential new patients. For example, phones like iPhones and Androids offer a built-in calling feature. A person can tap on a listing and see a pop up that says, "call this number?" No need to type in the number. No need to go home and use a landline. Smartphones offer pop up buttons with your office phone number. One tap and the potential new patient can call your office. However, this is only likely to happen if you are in a top spot.

You might think, "This is just for restaurants and bars." While these businesses were the "first adopters," it is also useful for weight loss practices. Searchers who come across your listing will take note, especially if they see multiple listings of yours appear from several different platforms, but all with a local designation. They'll most likely think, "this weight loss practice is right near my office!" You want to leave that impression, enough that they will file it away for future reference. Better yet, maybe they'll act right away. I can't say it enough; you need to have a local presence! If you don't, a competitor who does will draw those new leads to their practice instead of yours.

This social / search hybrid we've been discussing also brings up another topic: word-of-mouth referrals. This is no longer limited to in-person conversations. Now, and increasingly as we move forward, "Word-of-mouth" will be a combination of social network influence, Google search listings, and close personal referrals.

Instead of letting Google decide who's first on a results list, people will cross-reference using their social network apps. We all want to know what our "friends" think, our co-workers, and our community. And, by "community," I mean anyone connecting on a social platform. Users are creating circles of people online with whom they share interests and values. These are people they trust to give them an opinion. If that trusted network has a positive view of your practice, it will go a long way toward pushing them in your direction.

Your interaction level, reviews, and presence on platforms like Facebook are crucial. More and more people will search their social networks in the same way they are now searching on Google and other search engines. Internet results pages will always influence decisions, but results from social networks will play an even more prominent role going forward.

People accept what friends and family say and take it very seriously. This is especially true when it comes to business or service recommendations. From a marketing perspective, it's a proven fact that people give more weight to opinions from friends and family than from any other source. As a result, this combo of social and search is going to be very influential. You need to keep an eye on it as the technology progresses.

Direct Mail

It may seem counterintuitive to put direct mail marketing, known as "snail mail," on a list of what to look for in the future! It hardly seems like something that belongs in the "What's Next" category. In terms of marketing, direct mail is older than dust. But there is a reason it's still here. There is tremendous potential in this segment of marketing, especially as the years roll on. Why? Look at the fashion industry. Everything always comes back, no matter how outdated it might be. Anything that has worked in the past is likely to return. Direct mail is making a comeback, precisely because of the lack of use.

Due to the scarcity of real mail, paper mail pieces are a great tool to add to your toolkit.

Sending a well designed direct mail piece now and then is a smart choice. While it should never be the only thing you rely on, it is part of our overall marketing strategies. If you already have direct mail campaigns built into your process, there are ways to reinforce and strengthen its effectiveness.

You can incorporate tools like Google My Business, Facebook, Twitter, and others. And, with the right call-to-action, you can encourage people to visit your website. If done well, a direct mail piece gives people an increased awareness of your practice and services and can be used to shift them into online awareness. For example, direct mailers can include a URL or bar code, which leads to a special offer. Include a number they can text to get a unique report. And, as I mentioned previously, direct mail postcards are a great way to solicit reviews.

There are a lot of untapped direct mail options, methods that very few practices are using. If you incorporate them, you'll be ahead of the curve.

Texting

As I've just mentioned, direct mail creates an opportunity for potential new patients to receive snail mail with a phone number they can text for more information or a special offer. When they do, they immediately enter your marketing funnel. If the system is set up correctly, their text to you will trigger an autoresponder. They will instantly receive a follow-up text, an email, or a voicemail, and eventually, whatever you have promised to send.

If a new patient puts in their mobile phone number, send something like this: "Hi! We've just received your information. Thank you! Check your inbox for an email that includes a link to a free special report on weight loss success. We'll be in touch." Some folks in the restaurant/bar business have set up automatic text messaging to send out coupons or special offers.

Depending on your niche market, it's worth exploring whether a tactic that includes texting works for your audience. Once a potential new patient has given you their mobile number don't be afraid to send out texts once or twice a month. Make sure the messages are useful and don't send messages more often than that. It will be considered spam, the death knell for a relationship built on trust. Texts get read more than 90% of the time; Email can't make that claim. Some experts estimate that emails get read, on average, 17 to 20% of the time. A well-placed, well-timed text now and then can support your efforts to get new patients to call your office.

Direct Voicemail

Direct voicemail is when you send a voice message directly to a mobile phone without the owner hearing it ring or seeing it come in. This approach works very well. You want to avoid catching someone with a "live" call at the wrong time.

The systems designed for this purpose are innovative and can be pre-programmed with an outbound message. Send any kind of info but avoid making it too heavy on advertising. Host and promote a free event and invite them via phone. There are endless uses for direct to voicemail calls but use them sparingly. Reserve this tool for when there is something very important or unique.

Warning: We've seen practices discover tools for robocalling and use them to death, only to get reported as a spam account and lose their audience.

What makes for a compelling message? It should be no more than thirty to ninety seconds long and sent directly to voicemail, not sent as a live call. The voicemail notifier will pop up, but the phone won't ring. The potential new patient will see that there is a message and will listen to it when convenient. It's not intrusive, so the listening rate is much higher.

We highly recommend collecting mobile phone numbers from "warm" leads. It opens up this texting opportunity and a direct voicemail option. Direct voicemail allows you a chance to be highly personal, which is more effective. Use this method for special events or to promote local happenings relative to your practice. For example, if you decide to host a free seminar about weight loss or offer a complimentary service, like a blood pressure check-up, you can generate interest.

A personal invitation to the event, directly from you, the expert, is a great way to entice people to attend and learn more. This is a comfortable, friendly way for potential new patients to get to know you and develop a sense of trust, a big win.

Nothing is more critical to the success of practice than implementing a system that builds and communicates with a growing contact list. An ever-expanding email list = a thriving practice.

Very few practices do this, even though it can contribute to an effortless boost in new patient appointments, often as much as 25% every month. Why not? Although it is impossible to go back in time and find the people a practice has lost touch with, it is possible to adopt a new philosophy moving forward. Understand that every point of contact with a new person matters from now on.

Trending Topics

Staying on top of the evolutions in the industry is critical. We make it our job to track all of the latest news, trends, and tactics, so our clients are always well informed. Be sure to visit the link provided at the end of this chapter that will take you to our online space with all of the latest up-to-date information about digital marketing and its technology.

We called this chapter "What's Next" because the technologies and tools that relate to online marketing change rapidly. Some of these ideas and strategies that we've talked about are already coming into play. We're launching tests for our more forward-thinking clients, especially those operating in very competitive markets. We're helping them stay ahead of the curve.

The ideas included in this book are not theories or marketing "fluff." They're real strategies that have been implemented, tracked, and are working to bring in new patients for our client's practices. As we branch out and take our client's online marketing to the next level, we hope you will join us. Even if you haven't stayed abreast of this kind of marketing before, it's not too late. Begin your research now, get up to speed on all of the latest developments, and start implementing!

Because you have this guide, you now have an opportunity to visit our website to gain access to free information and all of the latest tips and trends. This information will be continuously updated, so be sure to check back often.

Just visit our website https://clinicmarketinggroup.com, and you'll find research, case studies, and plenty of valuable information about how to experience online marketing success and business growth.

Last Pro Tip: If your current marketing person or "team" doesn't seem to understand the techniques in this book, it might be time to make a change.

These methods are not well understood by most web designers or office staff who haven't worked with these tools in-depth. As things get more competitive, you need experienced, highly skilled help, someone who understands the full scope Internet marketing represents. But also someone focused intently on revenue growth. You can love what you do, but if you're not profitable doing it, there's no path to success.

I would love to create that path for your practice.

For more support, be sure to visit our website:
https://clinicmarketinggroup.com

Chapter 13: Getting IT Done

How to Hire the Right Outside Help

The final thing to discuss is resources, the workforce, and the financial capital needed to get real results.

Let's face it; you didn't kill yourself getting through med school, get licensed, and open the doors of your practice to spend 12 non-billable hours a day as a marketing person. This is a recipe for disaster. Any new patient you get will likely not return if this is the case. They will sense that the practice isn't being run by the practitioner, with their full attention on customer service and meeting the patient's needs. Do you want to spend your time making and uploading videos, submitting updated information to hundreds of directory listings, and poring over the code in your new website? Do you want to be up in the middle of the night, troubleshooting a site that has gone down?

Finding an expert that is affordable, and who can handle everything involved, isn't easy. Thousands of people have tried to teach themselves the ins and outs of online marketing, and the results they get are as superficial as their knowledge. Most web designers don't care or aren't aware of what results-driven online marketing looks like. They only care about design and basic website functionality. They're in love with the look of a website, rather than seeking to understand what you need it to accomplish.

I've seen clients hand over small but hard-earned payments to someone working out of a basement. I've seen others spend tens of thousands to a high-end agency, only to see the project drag out for an entire year. Eventually, the effort gets so bogged down, nothing launches.

The result of all of these scenarios is little to no change in practice profitability. I caution you to analyze carefully any investment you make in SEO or marketing. I get asked all the time how to find a good web designer. The answer is, who cares? If they don't know how to launch a site that registers and ranks with Google and converts traffic into new patients, what's the point?

Trying to get a website designed on the cheap doesn't work. Outsourcing to India or to someplace halfway around the world doesn't work. Having your new medical assistant who loves "doing this kind of work on the side," doesn't work. Hiring a fly-by-night business you heard from by phone and whom you've never met, doesn't work.

What does work?

Getting IT Done

By now, I hope you will agree that local web-based marketing is an extremely urgent, time-sensitive issue for your practice. It should be a top business priority. Every so often, a practitioner reaches out and asks for help. As they share their story, I imagine what their practice would look like if I had met them six to eighteen months ago. If they had allowed us to craft and implement an online marketing strategy for them, they would now be running a growing, thriving health clinic. They would own a professional and profitable practice.

But, today is still a great day to get started!

The decisions you make right now can positively impact your business in just a few short months. And, by this time next year, who knows? You might be a proud practitioner running a well-respected, profitable weight loss practice that helps people get healthier and live better lives.

A Failure to Act

Internet marketing is still a land of opportunity. This door is WIDE open. I'm no fortune teller, but, in my twenty years as an online marketing consultant, there is one thing I can predict with certainty. The opportunities you have right now to stake your claim in search results will lessen the longer you wait.

I don't want you to miss out on securing a profitable financial future just because you don't understand how online marketing works, or you don't have the time or resources to invest. You may not have thought online marketing was important. I hope this book has convinced you how critical Internet marketing is to the success of your practice because it is. I would love to share with you a bit more about how we operate because it could save us both time. While I would like to offer our services a la carte and allow clients to choose specific services off of a "menu," we simply can't.

Here's why:

The development and implementation of a comprehensive, full-court press marketing strategy is the only thing that truly works. It is the best way for my clients to see a return on their investment quickly. As soon as they see an increase in new business, they know their investment is worthwhile, and will soon be profitable. That's important to me. We prefer to build your online presence from the ground up, using every tool available to attract new contacts and turn them into recurring weight loss patients. My promise is that we will use every approach, device, and platform needed to grow your practice, the only path to a successful online marketing strategy.

Full disclosure: my clients, sign up for and receive turn-key, full-service marketing. Ours is a 100% Do-It-For-You service model. In my years of experience, I have found this to be the only way to guarantee that things are set up correctly. Once a contract is signed, our clients turn over the keys, and we do the rest. We've discovered that there are many people "interested" in online marketing in a general way. They believe that a little bit of knowledge goes a long way, when, in fact, the exact opposite is true. I wish I had $100 for every time a practitioner or business owner has gone into their website or social accounts to "try and make some changes." I'd be rich! Nine times out of nine, they blow the whole thing up. Rankings tank, site visibility, drops, site functions disappear. This means hours and hours of hard work down the drain.

I don't mean to sound disrespectful, but I would never allege that since I am interested in medicine, I should dabble in being a weight loss doctor. It works the other way, too. Just because you may have an interest in online marketing and technology doesn't mean you can match the 20 years of knowledge and experience my team has.

What I can say with certainty is that together, we can devise an online marketing plan that will get you better results than you ever thought possible at a reasonable cost compared to the new business it will bring in.

My service fees are not as low as someone who does limited work, like posting on Instagram. But, we do charge far less than full-scale agencies. With our business model, you only pay for what works. If given a choice between A. investing a small amount in something that has no impact on your business growth, or B. investing in efforts that brings hundreds of new patients into your practice, which will you choose? That will say a lot about whether we should work together. To be honest, I'm not interested in working with any practitioner that chooses A over B; it wouldn't be worth it for either of us.

As a professional that sincerely cares about my clients, I won't commit to having too many weight loss practitioners in a geographic area. There are two reasons for this. First, the quality of the content suffers because it becomes challenging to produce fresh, original content unique to each client. Second, I don't want clients competing with each other. I would be working against my own success and sacrificing yours.

So, be aware that we might not be free to entertain inquiries in specific markets. However, if, after working your way through this manual, you decide you would like to explore our services and inquire about our availability, give me a call. I'd love to hear from you.

Phone: (646) 969-3222
Email: Tim@clinicmarketinggroup.com
Web: https://clinicmarketinggroup.com

DISCLAIMER: Not all consultants are experts. If you pass this road map onto someone else, there is no guarantee you will see results. The truth is, you probably won't see results at all.

If the information in this book has been helpful, I'm glad. But, it would be irresponsible of me not to give you this small warning. In the past 15 years, I have developed many automated processes and systems that are not available outside of my practice. And I can't be responsible for someone else's inability to understand and implement the strategies described in this book. My best clients are those who see the case studies, the data, and the opportunity for profitability and say yes. They practice long-term thinking, and they know they can't do it alone without a significant investment. If that's you, I'd love to hear from you.

The End & New Beginnings

Hey, you made it! You've worked your way through this entire complex online marketing guide. You're on the other side, hopefully with your faculties intact, and you are ready to take on the challenges of online marketing success!

Thank you for trusting me enough to read this guide. And, a special thanks to anyone that has implemented these strategies 100%. Hats off, the rewards are already on their way!

Chapter 14: Case Studies

Making A Case for Clinic Marketing Group

An excellent digital marketing strategy is transformative. It doesn't just bring new traffic to a website; it brings new people into a business. For a medical professional, the Clinic Marketing Group approach launches profitable, professional medical practices that doctors can be proud of.

Clinic Marketing Group has taken this journey with many clients over the years, many of whom were close to shutting their doors when we met them. Each practice had a different set of problems that needed solving, but there was one thing they had in common-they didn't believe that digital marketing could save their business. But, thanks to CMG, it has.

In one case, the business was stuck. Patient visits were dwindling, and expenses were rising. Now they have multiple sites, and they dominate in a medium-size market. In another instance, there was no real practice to speak of, just a few patients a week with no plan on how to keep from going under. This is now an incredibly busy practice in one of the largest cities in the US. Finally, in a third instance, a niche medical service that is hard to market got new messaging and a more targeted audience. Now, they get hundreds of calls from new patients every month. Of course, the increase in new business has created new challenges, like managing it all efficiently, but we're helping with that as well. What a nice problem to have! I invite you to read the Case Studies below and fill out our Discovery Form, so we can begin transforming your practice, right away.

Case Study 01:
The Experienced Weight Loss Doctor

A physician goes from seeing a few patients one day a week in a borrowed office to owning two thriving medical clinics.

When a physician contacted Clinic Marketing Group (CMG), the situation was dire. He was seeing a few patients each week in a rented office. After listening to deceptive SEO salespeople and hiring an expensive branding agency, the practice was out six figures in advertising costs, with no uptick in new patient calls.

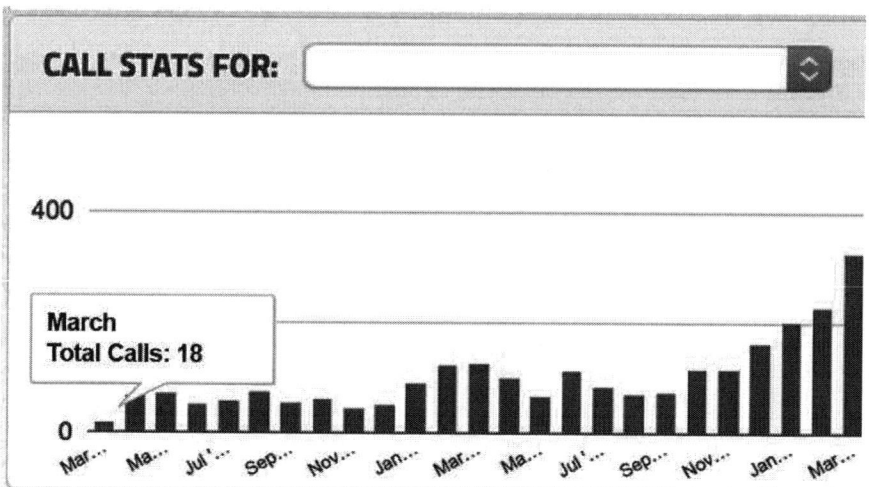

CALL STATS FOR:

400

March
Total Calls: 18

0

Mar··· Ma··· Jul··· Sep··· Nov··· Jan··· Mar··· Ma··· Jul··· Sep··· Nov··· Jan··· Mar···

Starting Inbound Call Flow

Incoming Calls Month One: 18
Peak Monthly Calls: 690
Annual New Patient Revenue (Est.): $1,386,000

The Initial Consultation

During the initial consultation, we posed some tough questions. Are you calculating cost-per-new-patient when you make an ad spend? Do you train staff on how to convert a phone inquiry into an appointment? Have you gained new business by buying listings, radio ads, or pay-per-click campaigns? The answer to these questions was no.

We designed a comprehensive marketing plan, launched a well-designed, correctly coded website, and ran ongoing social media, email, and "special offer" campaigns. We also unleashed a few secret weapons unique to CMG. Today, this practitioner owns two successful medical clinics.

Our Solution

Clinic Marketing Group develops a monthly plan of attack for every client, ongoing tasks that push businesses into the top spots in search results, and helps them stay there.

Our reputation marketing helped this practice collect dozens of positive patient reviews, which got published on strategic sites. Next, we coached staff on how to turn inquiries into appointments. We worked hard to help them increase their efficiency and profitability. And, we tracked new patient calls each month.

Reputation Marketing

A part-time practice turns into two thriving clinics generating $2.7 million in two years; that's a Success Metric. Reputation Marketing is one of the ways we helped them get there.

Reputation Marketing Video and Social Media Campaign

Clinic Marketing Group initiated our Reputation Marketing process to manage, build, and market authentic, positive patient reviews. These were submitted to sites deemed strategically useful to drive results. Anyone searching the Internet is now more likely to find this practice, and when they do, they find a reputable, professional provider with five-star ratings. No other marketing tool inspires action more than positive patient reviews.

Social Media Marketing

Rather than produce superficial social media activity, CMG penetrates the Internet deeply with great content that drives practices up into search results and triggers new patient calls.

We got this practice broad exposure for original, Google-approved news articles, blog posts, special offers, video testimonials we created. These efforts brought qualified traffic to the website and inspired phone calls for inquiries and appointments.

Social Media and Reputation Marketing Campaign

This practice went from invisible, to dominating in their market for search results. By the end of the first year, this physician received an average of 400 new patient calls every month.

Traffic Campaigns

This practice needed us to generate results as quickly as possible. Campaigns were designed with that in mind and sent to CMG's extensive network of media outlets. When qualified traffic found the clinic's site, they also saw call-to-action banners or a portal to sign up for a free report.

Campaigns included the phrases people were using most often to search and included positive patient testimonials, special offers, and local news articles. We help them reach hundreds of thousands of potential new patients. This clinic shows up at the top of search results for seven key search phrases and gets a steady stream of new patient calls.

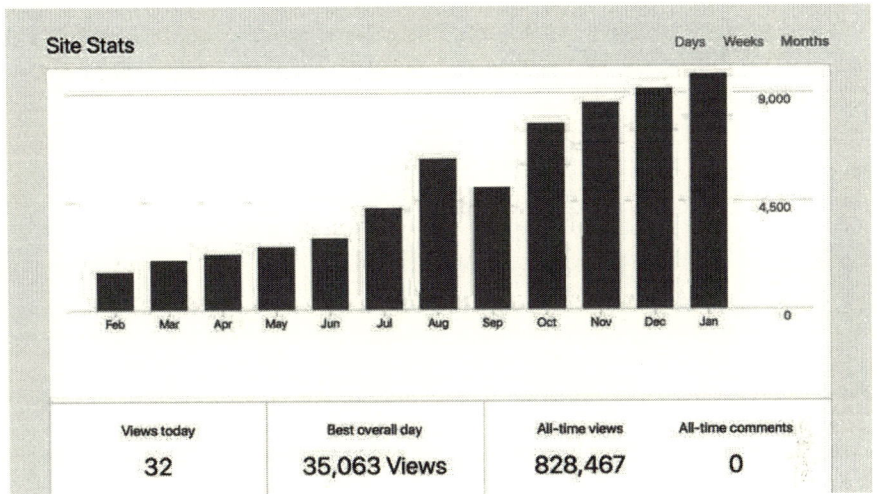

Monthly Website Traffic Increase

Advanced Analytics

Clinic Marketing Group is about establishing business growth objectives and working tirelessly to achieve them. Our advanced analytics are what help us achieve those goals for your business.

Getting ranked highly in search results and seeing an increase in new calls to a practice takes expertise and hours of hard work. There is nothing more disappointing than calls not turning into new patient appointments. We determine the cost-per-patient of the marketing we do, and we'll discover the fastest path to profitability, something rare in the digital marketing world. We track all of the traffic and new business going to this practice and send a Success Metric report every month.

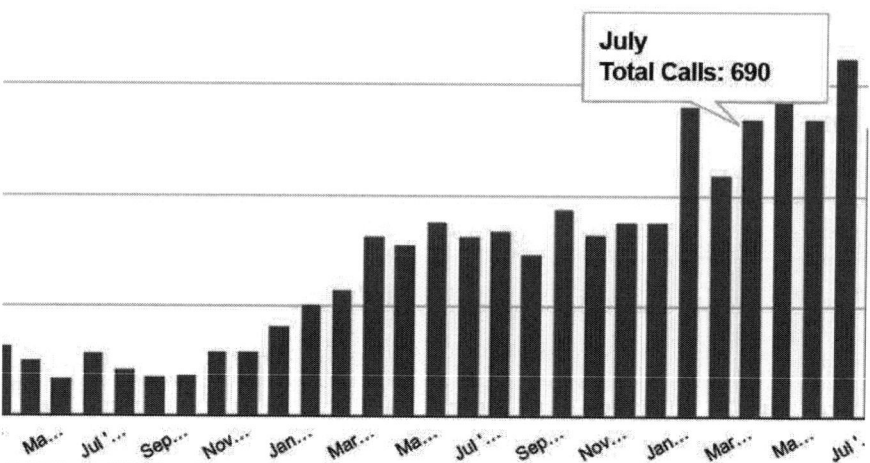

Inbound Call Flow INcrease from 18 Calls to 690 Calls a Month

Case Study 02:

The Physician Turned Weight Loss Doctor

A fill-in physician, tired of the rat race, finds a new life by opening a profitable medical weight loss practice.

Discouraged, this doctor was down to seeing tops, five patients a week, in a borrowed office. Skeptical that anything would change, he was willing to discuss the challenge of finding new patients one last time before giving up.

Clinic Marketing Group knew we had to work with urgency, so we launched a jump start strategy to help his practice rise quickly in search results, and layered in our reputation management so that people would see five-star reviews. Now a digital marketing convert, this doctor welcomes at least fifteen new patients every week and is hopeful about the future.

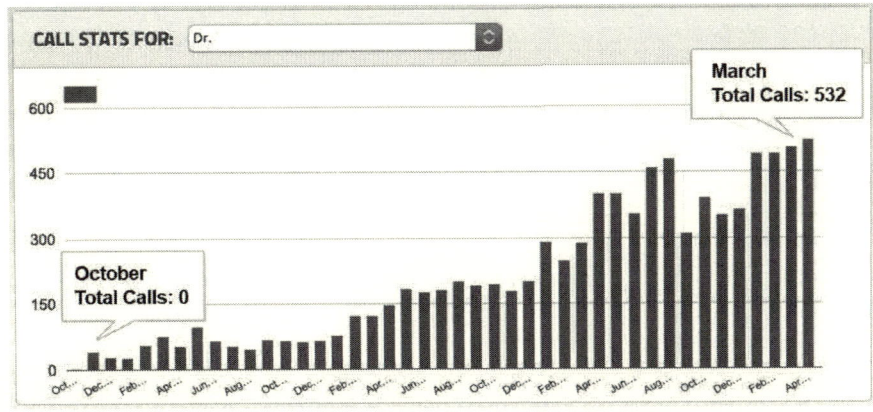

Campaign Call Stats - 5 Calls a Month to 532 Calls a Month

Incoming Calls Month One: 5
Peak Monthly Calls: 532
Annual New Patient Revenue (Est.): $1,020,000

Initial Consultation

During the initial consultation, it was clear that this doctor had no marketing plan, no approach for seeking referrals, and no protocol for welcoming new patients. He didn't have a functional understanding of how to use social media and grow his practice.

Radical changes in digital marketing and consumer behavior have left many doctors like this one stranded. Over 97% of people who seek healthcare services search online before making a decision. Once the doctor understood that, without an online presence, his practice didn't exist, he was ready for change.

Our Solution

Clinic Marketing Group went full throttle on a comprehensive digital marketing strategy, pulling new people in and inspiring them to take action by scheduling a medical weight loss appointment.

We built a modest, well-organized website, and followed up with a comprehensive social media assault. We invested in both traffic driven and "special offer" campaigns. We also launched a Reputation Marketing effort so patients could submit positive reviews and create an aura of trust.

These efforts didn't just generate traffic; they generated new patient calls, about 400 every month.

Reputation Marketing

Studies show that people trust the information they find online. But, for a medical practice that online presence must be impeccable. That's what our Reputation Marketing service does; it creates a sense of professionalism, combined with compassion.

CMG coached the doctor's new staff on how to ask for patient reviews and provided branded Review Request cards to hand out, making it easier. In addition to influencing a better ranking, the positive reviews this doctor receives tells newcomers that this is a medical practice they can trust.

Social Media Marketing

Activity-based marketing is vastly different from a comprehensive social media plan. The first earns you a few "likes" on Facebook, the other pushes your practice to the top of search results and brings in new business.

Clinic Marketing Group created a wealth of new, original content for the practice, and syndicated it widely. The doctor's listing has positive patient reviews, videos, and gets seen by thousands of potential new patients living in his region, every day.

Traffic Campaigns

Our campaigns for the practice incorporate carefully identified key phrases, words that people use to search for weight loss services every day. We have a vast network of media outlets and platforms, all hungry for new content that people will click-on to learn more. The website is well-organized, inspires trust, and triggers visitors to act. The practice has seen an increase of about 25% to 33% in new patient calls every month.

CMG writes compelling copy, informative blog posts, and we produce and publish video testimonials. Potential new patients find plenty of reasons to call this practice for medical weight loss support. Digital marketing like this does work, and we have the Success Metrics to prove it.

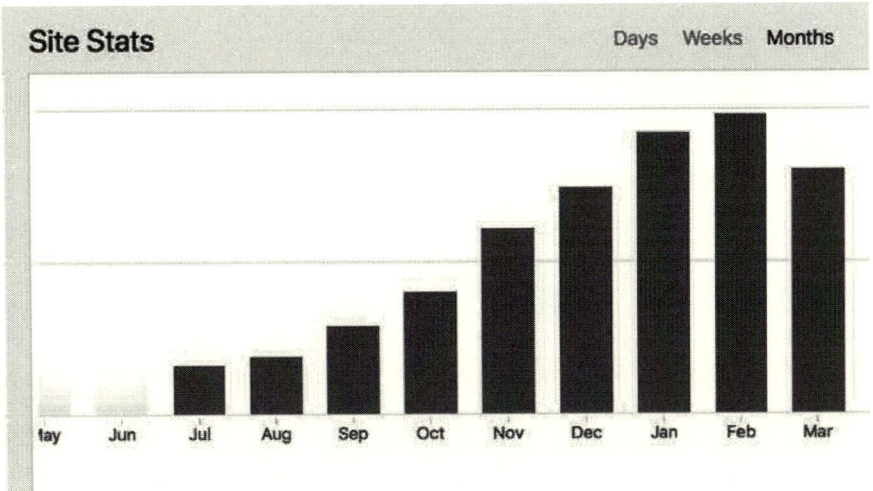

Monthly Website Traffic Increase

Advanced Analytics

This practice spent so many years without new patient calls; the office wasn't ready to handle them or provide an excellent customer experience.

So, we sent a script and coached staff on how to shift from giving information to asking for appointments. We helped them streamline patient scheduling and analyze what each new patient was worth to the practice overall. Their conversion rate and retention rate increased drastically once these changes were implemented. Not only did this doctor's patient flow increase, so did his profitability.

Case Study 03:
The Holistic Medical Doctor

A medical doctor with a holistic approach has few patients and struggles to become profitable.

Despite a small band of loyal patients, this doctor was barely covering expenses, let alone a personal income. He had a superficial understanding of what social media could accomplish. After hiring a part-time SEO person, the phone still wasn't ringing, a serious disappointment. Clinic Marketing Group created a scalable digital marketing strategy that generates calls from 300+ new people every month.

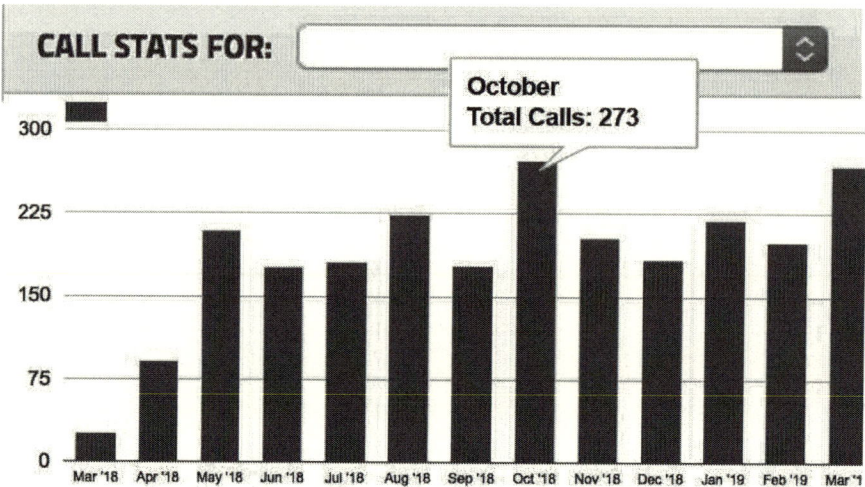

Inbound Call Flow to Medical Practice from 5 Calls a Month to 273 Calls a Month

Incoming Calls Month One: 5
Peak Monthly Calls: 273
Annual New Patient Revenue (Est.): $1,462,500

Initial Consultation

A medical practitioner trained in two medical disciplines can hardly be expected to master digital marketing too. Our initial conversation revealed a lot of gaps in this doctor's expectations of what superficial social media could do. We let him know that Clinic Marketing Group is not about useless SEO "busy work," but smart strategies, hard work, and ongoing creative content production that results in new patient calls.

Once we clearly defined what made this practitioner unique, we tailored an ambitious digital strategy and got to work.

Our Solution

Clinic Marketing Group developed a modest, more personalized website that registers with search engines and gives visiting traffic a sense of trust regarding his professionalism and compassion. CMG's ongoing monthly marketing plan keeps the practice at the top of search results in the local market, with an online presence that encourages people to call. Publishing positive reviews from his loyal patient base, and implementing in-office systems for increased efficiency and profitability, round out our services.

This once skeptical practitioner now has the challenge of managing a steady increase in calls every month, and caring for hundreds of new patients.

Reputation Marketing

Planting in a big city means expenses are high, and profitability is often an issue. This doctor needed an influx of new patients willing to pay out-of-pocket for his unique gifts as a holistic medical doctor providing excellent, personalized care.

Clinic Marketing Group tapped into his existing loyal patient base. The CMG Reputation Marketing kit made it easy for his practice to gather glowing patient reviews, and we added these to the sterling online reputation we were building for him. He now presents as the number one integrative medicine doctor in this metropolitan area.

Social Media Marketing

Engaging a new audience for the practice and drawing them closer required an intense focus on getting the content right. This practitioner integrates medical science and prescription medications and natural, organic treatments when appropriate. Informative insights in traditional medicine blended with trends in holistic medicine in the articles, blog posts, and videos we created.

Accounts on social channels were opened and linked. Our vast network allowed us to distribute content to a broad but targeted audience. This approach contributed to a significant rise in search engine rankings and led hundreds of new patients to call the practice every month.

Traffic Campaigns

Traffic campaigns open a direct line between our clients and their potential new customers, as social media sites allow us to put out special offers to entice new people to act, rather than just read.

The search campaigns for this practitioner required expertise in keyword selection. After studying analytics and consumer behavior, we carefully integrated organic SEO with paid traffic to increase his reach. This comprehensive, yet cost-effective approach to traffic generation delivered pre-qualified audiences to the web site, with a higher rate of people taking action and calling the practice.

Advanced Analytics

Clinic Marketing Group worked with this practitioner to streamline the office procedure for handling the significant uptick in inbound calls from new patients. There needs to be a balance between providing information and getting the appointment booked.

Our virtual consulting service coached this practice on managing new patient calls, the front desk, and scheduling issues to ensure that patients have an excellent experience, start to finish. These coaching sessions are challenging but a unique opportunity to increase patient retention and profitability. This doctor has a full roster of appointments every day and is considering a second location.

Appendix 1

Analytics: Analytics are technical measures you can take to see what happens with visitors on your website: how long they stay, what they click, how many of them return to the site, and statistics of that nature. One of the best analytic software packages out there currently is Google Analytics, which is also free.

Autoresponder: An autoresponder is a system put in place to automatically respond to communication initiated by a potential client, usually via email. Autoresponders can range from simple to complex. They can send one generic email, or users choose from dozens of templates. What gets sent depends on the form used or the information provided by the client.

Bing: A major search engine, like Google and Yahoo. It has many of the same features and has the next-largest market share of any of the search engines after Google.

Blog: Originally an abbreviation of the term "weblog," it now means a type of website (or part of a website) frequently updated with new content. It has many interactive options for users to leave comments and otherwise participate. Many blogs are powered by software explicitly designed to make this frequent updating easier, like WordPress or Typepad.

Call-to-Action: Content on a website or other communication that appeals to the reader to contact the business.

CRM: An acronym for "Customer Relationship Management." In the context of Internet marketing, it most often refers to the software that manages patients and potential patients of the business, such as names, locations, likes, dislikes, needs, and other relevant information.

Directory: In the sense of Internet marketing, a website or part of a website whose purpose is to list businesses. Some, like Yelp, Merchant Circle, or CitySearch, feature user-generated business reviews.

Duplicate Content: Identical content that appears on multiple websites. Search engines have algorithms to detect this, even if the material has been only slightly altered. Duplicate (stolen) content that is flagged must be removed.

E-Commerce: The buying and selling of products and services over the Internet.

Facebook: A social networking site that is currently the most popular in the world; it allows users to network with each other and socialize, including sharing photos, thoughts, status updates, and wall posts with each other.

Facebook Places: Shows users local spots that are nearby, and allows them to update their location in real-time using their mobile phone or device so that others can see where they are.

Geolocation: In Internet marketing and SEO, a term used to describe location-specific information, such as city and state, for local businesses.

Google Maps: A part of Google's website that primarily deals with maps and navigation. This feature allows local businesses to list their location in the Google Maps services, but it also factors them into main search results.

Google Places: A part of Google's website that allows a business to have a dedicated page. It connects with a location on Google Maps, features user-generated reviews and links to other directory listings or review sites.

IP Address: A unique number that identifies a computer on a network.

Keyword: A phrase that a user searches with in a search engine to retrieve content that contains, or is relevant to, the term.

Keyword Density: The use of a specific keyword present in any given piece of content. For example, given the keyword "racing" used five times in a 500-word blog post, the keyword density of "racing" would be 1%. Optimal keyword density is between 3 and 4% and should not exceed 4%, or it may be flagged as spam.

Long Tail Keyword Phrase: A phrase composed of individual words but treated as a single keyword for a search, like "Nascar car racing" or "racing opportunities in Texas."

Keyword-Rich: Content that has many keywords and uses them often, with good keyword density.

Keyword Tool:: Tools to help select optimal keywords for search engine marketing, like Google's Keyword Tool. They contain information such as the amount of searches for a particular keyword or other metrics that help determine how popular or prevalent a keyword phrase is.

LinkedIn: A social networking site geared toward businesses and professionals, enabling them to link up and network more effectively.

Local Search Results: A feature within Google's search engine that returns specific results for users based on their location. For example, a local search return might appear for a user in Omaha, Nebraska who types in "law firm elder law." A map and any business relevant to the search term may appear in results.

Niching: The practice of specializing a marketing strategy to a certain keyword or keyword phrase in order to rank in the highest spot in a local search returns for that keyword or keyword phrase.

ROI: An acronym for "Return on Investment," which means the amount of profit; in literal terms, the amount of money returned for the amount of money invested.

Search Algorithm: A series of computer algorithms used by major search engines to index, search, and rank websites on the Internet.

Search Engine: A website or company, like Google, Bing, or Yahoo, that indexes other websites on the Internet and allows users to enter keywords in order to find relevant websites.

SEO: An acronym for "Search Engine Optimization" SEO refers to the practice of marketing to increase exposure and clientele by using techniques to rank high on Internet search engine results. Might also be referred to as SEM (Search Engine Marketing).

Social Media: Sites whose primary purpose is to enable users to share content and socialize on the Internet; examples include Facebook, Twitter, and LinkedIn. In marketing terms the general practice of using social platforms to connect with customers.

Spam: Originally unsolicited bulk messages sent over email, SPAM is defined more broadly as useless content whose sole purpose is to trick search engine algorithms into ranking a page higher.

Tweet: An individual post on Twitter, limited to 280 characters.

Twitter: A social networking service that allows users to post tweets (see "Tweets" above) to their account, with the ability for other users to follow them and respond to the tweets.

Unique Selling Position (USP): The aspect of a business that sets it apart from competitors that offer similar products or services. Often highlighted as the primary focus of a marketing strategy.

URL: An acronym for "Uniform Resource Locator." URL is the string of letters and symbols used to identify a website on the Internet. Users type these unique identifiers into a browser bar of search engines to access specific sites (i.e., "www.google.com" or "www.bing.com").

About the Author

Tim McGarvey is a "Growth Strategist" that believes in developing long term, practical marketing strategies for his clients that helps them achieve their business goals.

A pioneer of online marketing tools since 1989, Tim's pet peeve: superficial "feel good" social media tactics that alleviate the anxiety of not "doing enough online," but accomplish little when it comes to bringing new business in the door.

His battle tested strategies and systems are thoughtful, sustainable, and measurable.

Rather than sell flashy, sexy approaches to Internet marketing, Tim builds long term relationships with his clients, who trust him to utilize his deep understanding of Internet marketing to grow their business over time, and achieve their life goals.

Tim lives in New York City with his wife, three teenagers, and is a part-time dog owner who enjoys running, racquetball and building five star reputations for his client's online.

Invite Us To Speak At Your Next Event

Want us to speak at your next event?

Our programs are designed to optimize online marketing strategies for weight loss practices. Our agency focuses on advanced SEO (Search Engine Optimization) and Local Search as an alternative means to traditional marketing.